THE WAR
AGAINST
THE TERROR
MASTERS

ALSO BY MICHAEL A. LEDEEN

Tocqueville on American Character

Machiavelli on Modern Leadership

Freedom Betrayed

Superpower Dilemmas

D'Annunzio: The First Duce

Perilous Statecraft

Debacle: Carter and the Fall of the Shah

Italy in Crisis

Universal Fascism

West European Communism and American Foreign Policy

THE WAR AGAINST THE TERROR MASTERS

Why It Happened. Where We Are Now. How We'll Win.

MICHAEL A. LEDEEN

TRUMAN TALLEY BOOKS
ST. MARTIN'S GRIFFIN
NEW YORK

www.stmartins.com

Library of Congress Cataloging-in-Publication Data

Ledeen, Michael Arthur, 1941–
    The war against the terror masters : why it happened, where we are now, how we'll win / Michael A. Ledeen.—1st St. Martin's Griffin ed.
        p. cm.
    "Truman Talley books."
    Includes bibliographical references and index.
    Contents: The rise of the terror network — The home front — The foreign theater — How to win the war — Final thoughts — Looking forward.
    ISBN 0-312-30644-X (hc)
    ISBN 0-312-32043-4 (pbk)
    1. War on Terrorism, 2001– 2. Terrorism—United States—Prevention.
3. Intelligence service—United States. 4. Terrorism—Middle East.
5. Islamic fundamentalism. I. Title.

HV6432.L43 2003
973.931—dc21

                                                                2003046839

First St. Martin's Griffin Edition: September 2003

10 9 8 7 6 5 4 3 2 1

This book is dedicated to Colonel Tom O'Connell (U.S. Army, retired), who did a tough tour in Vietnam, played a key role in shaping intelligence for U.S. Special Forces, and was an original member of the Office of Military Affairs at the C.I.A. With ten of him we'd easily thrash the terror network with one hand tied behind our backs. But there couldn't be ten of him. One is already a miracle.

CONTENTS

INTRODUCTION

The fact is that America is a special country, my dear friend. A country to envy, of which to be jealous . . .

—ORIANA FALLACI

One morning in early 1996, shortly after he became President Clinton's second director of central intelligence, John Deutch came to the American Enterprise Institute for a quiet breakfast with a handful of AEI's intelligence and foreign policy experts, including Richard Perle and Jeane Kirkpatrick. It was a fairly routine event. Deutch wanted to get some ideas, and, as most everyone in Washington is engaged in politics most all the time, he wanted to convince us that even Clinton's DCI might be worthy of our support (most AEI scholars had been unimpressed with the administration's approach to world affairs).

He outlined his priorities for about ten minutes, and then asked for some feedback. At my turn, I told him I was surprised that the task for which the CIA had been created—providing the country with timely warning of any sudden attack like Pearl Harbor—was not on his list, and I wondered if that had been an oversight or a deliberate change of priorities. He assured us it was not an oversight. The world had changed, and, with the fall of the Soviet empire, we no longer had to devote a lot of talent and energy to worrying about a surprise military attack. There just wasn't anyone out there who could threaten us as had Nazi Germany, Imperial Japan, and the Soviet Union.

Deutch was not alone in believing that America was secure for the foreseeable future, nor was the Clinton administration uniquely shortsighted in this regard. The first President Bush permitted himself the observation that, in the post–Cold War world, threats to the United States would be economic, not military. This view was widely shared inside the government and throughout the intellectual community, above all by the prophets of globalization, many of whom went so far as to predict that the nation–state itself would soon become irrelevant, and thus the very idea of "national security" would become an historical curiosity.

So when we ask ourselves how we could have failed to see that our enemies were preparing to attack us on September 11, 2001, and why we were so poorly prepared to defend ourselves, we have to begin by recognizing that our failure was very broad and very deep, and that our leaders simply refused to see what was going on. Of course, the terrorists tried to hide their activities from us, and there is certainly no guarantee that we would have detected them even if John Deutch had put "no new Pearl Harbors" at the top of his mission statement. But we afforded the terrorists every opportunity to succeed in their murderous activities. Aside from a handful of experts—most of whom were written off as congenital "hawks" or "Cold Warriors," or could be dismissed as professional practitioners of counterterrorism and thus had a personal career interest in selling fear of terrorism to those who could pay for their advice and expertise—hardly anyone in a position of political, governmental or intellectual authority seriously contemplated a major assault against American civilians within the United States.

The conventional wisdom was summed up in an op-ed article in *The New York Times* on July 10, 2001—almost exactly two months before the attack—

by one Larry C. Johnson, a former State Department counterterrorism specialist. The basic sermon was simple: There's really nothing much to worry about. ". . . If you are drilling for oil in Colombia—or in nations like Ecuador, Nigeria, or Indonesia," Mr. Johnson wrote, "you should take appropriate precautions; otherwise Americans have little to fear."

He predicted that terrorism would decline in the decade beginning in 2000, as it had in the nineties primarily because of "the current reluctance of countries like Iraq, Syria, and Libya, which once eagerly backed terrorist groups, to provide safe havens, funding and training."

Finally, Mr. Johnson blamed the inflated fear of terrorism on "24-hour broadcast news operations too eager to find a dramatic story" and on "pundits who repeat myths while ignoring clear empirical data," along with politicians who "warn constituents of dire threats and then appropriate money for redundant military installations and new government investigators and agents." To round out his rogues' gallery, Mr. Johnson criticized the military and intelligence bureaucracies, "desperate to find an enemy to justify budget growth."

The fundamental error in this reasoning was an old one: the assumption that the near future would resemble the immediate past. Like the believers in stock charts and roulette systems, those who tracked the rhythms of international terror had assumed that the decline had established an ongoing pattern. There had indeed been a dropoff in terrorist activity in the nineties, because the defeat of the Soviet Union had deprived the terrorists of their major sponsor. But that, as we now know, did not mean that the other terror masters had gone into retirement. Of the three countries on Johnson's list, Libya had in fact reduced its support for terrorism, but Iraq and Syria certainly had not. And Iran, which Johnson's own State Department correctly identifies as the world's prime terror sponsor, was unaccountably left off his short list. Tehran's mullahs and ayatollahs relentlessly drove the terrorist campaign against us.

In any event, history only takes you so far, and even the great historians who wrote the Old Testament insisted that times always change. Nobody had attacked the United States since the War of 1812, but then came Pearl Harbor. Nobody had attacked the American mainland since the War of 1812 either, but then came September 11. National leaders are supposed to protect us against worst-case scenarios, not spend their time with futurologists. We don't want past-is-prologue philosophy, we want security. But the mission was gutted, at precisely the moment of our greatest power relative to the rest of the world. We forgot Machiavelli's dictum that "man is more inclined to do evil than to do good," and we indulged ourselves in happier thoughts for more than a decade.

Fool me once, shame on you, goes the schoolyard

chant, but fool me twice, shame on me. We were fooled many times, to our leaders' great shame. Looking back at the long history of terrorist assaults against Americans and American targets, reading the hate-filled rantings of the terrorists and the leaders of the terror states, it seems utterly incredible that our government did not realize what was underway. There are many pages ahead dealing with our remarkable intelligence failures, but, as is so often the case, one really didn't need sensitive intelligence to recognize the steady growth of the terrorist threat. You might not know the cave address for Osama bin Laden on a given date, but anyone who followed Middle East affairs knew that he was a true fanatic, had lots of money, and had trained many followers quite prepared to die for their mission—which was to kill as many Americans as they could. That knowledge should have driven us to act, and the decision to act would have driven the intelligence people to do their jobs. Without a mission, the intelligence community was doomed to failure.

It's like talking to a government lawyer: If you ask him whether or not you can do something, he'll err on the side of caution and warn you against it. But if you tell him you've decided to do something and instruct him to develop the strongest legal case for it, he will. The intelligence community focuses much better when it's supporting a real policy. If the president clearly has no intention of doing anything much anyway—and that was the case for at least a dozen years before George W. Bush—then the CIA had no reason to take any risks in order to come up with chapter and verse on Al Qaeda, Hizbollah, Hamas, the PLO, or Islamic Jihad. The Pentagon had no reason to design a strategy to destroy the terror masters who governed Middle Eastern countries, principally Iran, Iraq, and Syria. And the State Department certainly had no reason to come to grips with the complicated problem of Saudi Arabia. What were they supposed to do with a country that is simultaneously our major oil supplier and the main financier of our terrorist enemies? Saudi Arabia has worked long and hard to keep oil prices low, which is enormously helpful to us. But Saudi Arabia has also funded the worldwide network of radical Islamic schools that have bred a generation of fanatical anti-American terrorists.

So the primary failure was political, a lack of will to fight a real war against the terror masters. Without a policy commitment, the spies and the analysts took it easy, thereby closing the vicious circle. There was no policy to drive the intelligence, and the intelligence was insufficient to drive policy.

American Character

There were other causes, lodged deep in our national psyche. As Tocqueville observed in 1831, we are a bundle of contradictions, at once the most religious and the most secular, the most individualistic and the most socially conscious, the most isolationist and the most interventionist people on earth. Our unique dynamism is generated by these contradictions; they create an inner tension that drives American creativity.

Like few before us, we have only a very limited interest in the world outside our shores. We tend to our own affairs, and we have done it so successfully that we are the first people in history to believe peace is the normal condition of mankind. That is one of the two major reasons why we are never ready for the next war. Every time a war ends, we demobilize, believing war itself has been defeated. As far back as 1846, when we were on the verge of a two-front war that produced the expansion of the United States into Texas, California, and Oregon, the United States Congress was planning to shut down the military academy at West Point. We generally have to be dragged into war. In the twentieth century we were torpedoed into the first World War on the North Atlantic, bombed into the second World War in the Pacific, frightened into the Cold War by Stalin, and shocked into the Gulf War by Saddam Hussein. September 11 revealed that we had once again let down our guard, despite years of terrorist attacks against Americans within and beyond our borders. Our leaders largely ignored the terrorists and concentrated on the abundant good news from the stock markets and the polls.

The other reason we are never ready for war is our radical egalitarianism and our belief in the perfectibility of man. We think all people everywhere are fundamentally the same and, having turned the study of history into a hymn to the wonders of multiculturalism, we are reluctant to accept Machiavelli's dictum that man is more inclined to do evil than to do good. Throughout this generation of political correctness, it has been singularly bad form for anyone in America to suggest that there are some truly evil people, and even some thoroughly evil regimes, whose fear and hatred of us are so intractable that "live and let live" (our mind set) will not do. It has to be "kill or be killed."

Having understood our national character better than anyone else before or since, Alexis de Tocqueville warned that foreign policy was our Achilles' heel. Foreign policy requires patience and secrecy, while we are impulsive doers and cherish the openness of our society. It's difficult for us to sustain the quiet hard discipline that foreign affairs so often require.

Hence, we're vulnerable. The evildoer always gets

the first shot. But Tocqueville also recognized that we have an amazing capacity to pull together and to postpone our craving for personal success and private satisfaction until the common good has been safeguarded and advanced. "War almost always enlarges the mind of a people and raises their character," Tocqueville tells us, and "in some cases it is the only check to the excessive growth of certain (selfish) tendencies."[1] Just ask the Germans or the Japanese or the Soviets, or Mullah Omar and the other fallen leaders of the ruined Taliban, all of whom grossly underestimated our enormous capacity to rapidly unite to accomplish a national mission.

They are not alone; our national capacity to spontaneously organize ourselves to overcome challenges is hard to explain, even for an acute observer like Tocqueville. It is the mystery of American patriotism.

> How does it happen that in the United States, where the inhabitants have only recently immigrated . . . where they met one another for the first time with no previous acquaintance; where, in short, the instinctive love of country can scarcely exist; how does it happen that everyone takes as zealous an interest in the affairs of the whole state . . . as if they were his own?[2]

It is because we feel ourselves part of a common enterprise—the advance of freedom—and we spontaneously organize ourselves to achieve that enterprise.

Our national capacity to pull together was catalyzed by the attack of September 11. One of the few to understand this magical process is Oriana Fallaci, the celebrated Italian writer, a longtime thorn in the personae of the self-important, a fiery Tuscan who has become a proud New Yorker. She took four full pages of the *Corriere della Sera* to speak of the September events and our response to them. She was struck by the reaction at Ground Zero to President George W. Bush shortly after the catastrophe.

> All of them, young people, little kids, the old, and the middle-aged. White, black, yellow, brown, purple . . . Did you see them or not? While Bush thanked them they waved the American flags, raised their clenched fists, and roared, "USA! USA! USA!" In a totalitarian country I would have thought, "but look at how well the powerful have organized them!" In America, no. In America you don't organize these things. Especially in a cynical metropolis like New York. New York workers are tough guys, and freer than the wind. These guys even disobey their

trade unions. But if you touch the flag, if you touch the country . . .

The fact is that America is a special country, my dear friend. A country to envy, of which to be jealous . . . and it is that way because it is born of a spiritual necessity . . . and of the most sublime human idea: the idea of liberty, or better, of liberty married to the idea of equality . . . [3]

Oriana Fallaci is our friend, and she understands us very well. Our enemies don't, which is why they constantly make the mistake of striking at us before they can be sure they will take us out. Thus, the Japanese at Pearl Harbor. Thus, Saddam Hussein in Kuwait. Thus, Osama bin Laden in New York and Washington and Pennsylvania. They see our internal divisions, they see our drive for material comfort, they know our leaders dread the thought of body bags on television, and they think we are not capable of fighting back at them. They should listen to Tocqueville, who knew back in 1831 that once we are engaged in a fight, "the same passions that made them attach so much importance to the maintenance of peace will be turned to arms." The awesome power of a free society committed to a single mission is something they cannot imagine.

Our enemies have now seen the evidence in their

own streets, deserts, and mountain redoubts. Our unexpectedly quick and impressive victory in Afghanistan is a prelude to a much broader war, which will in all likelihood transform the Middle East for at least a generation, and reshape the politics of many other countries around the world.

The Nature of the War

The conventional mantra that the war on terrorism will be a totally new kind of war, unlike those we have fought in the past, is right about some of the details—we will have to defeat clandestine organizations as well as national armies, and we will have to fight at home as well as abroad—but it is true only in part. Our prime enemies are the terror masters—the rulers of the countries that sponsor terrorism, and the leaders and soldiers of the terrorist organizations themselves. The new part of the war concerns the structure of the terrorist organizations: They are organized in cells, not regular armies, and they hide themselves within civil society and attack innocent civilians pursuing normal activities, rather than setting themselves apart by wearing uniforms and attacking our armed forces on battlefields. But this is not a total innovation. We have had to deal with covert assassins and saboteurs in previous wars, and our intelligence community spent much of the Cold War fighting covert Soviet agents.

The main part of the war—the campaign against the terror masters who rule countries hostile to us—is a very old kind of war. It is a revolutionary war, right out of the eighteenth century, the very kind of war that gave us our national identity. While we will have to act against secret terrorist organizations and kamikaze fighters, our ultimate targets are tyrannical regimes. We will require different strategies in each case. We will need one method and set of tools to bring down Saddam Hussein, another strategy to break the Assad family dictatorship in Syria, a very different approach to end the religious tyranny in Iran, and yet another to deal with Saudi Arabia's active support for fundamentalist Islam and the terror network. But the mission is the same in each case: Bring down the terror masters.

There are those who say we are fighting a shadowy, elusive enemy. However, all of the major terrorist organizations would be crippled without state support. Once the terrorists are deprived of safe havens, training camps, sources of travel documents, the use of diplomatic pouches, and really secure communications, they will be easier pickings.

The United States defeated Japanese kamikazes over the Pacific Ocean during World War II in two ways: by improving our defenses, and by destroying the Tokyo regime. To win the war against the terror masters we will have to do the same: improve our homeland defense, kill or incarcerate the terrorist rank and file, and destroy the regimes that support the new kamikazes. As President Bush has said, the war has to be waged against the terrorists and the countries that support or harbor them.

This book attempts to put the war in context by answering three questions: Why did it happen? Where do we stand today? How will we win? A few explanatory words are in order.

—*Why it happened.* The first chapter recounts the history of the terror network, from the PLO through the Iranian Revolution, to Al Qaeda and the current threat. It includes an analysis of the importance of Islamic fundamentalism within the terror network, as well as the crucial roles of several Middle Eastern regimes.

But that is only part of the "why." The other part is "why weren't we properly prepared?" and that requires a detailed look at both American counterterrorist policy, and the performance of the intelligence agencies that are responsible for our national security: the Federal Bureau of Investigation (at home) and the Central Intelligence Agency (abroad). Those are the subjects of the second and third chapters.

—*Where do we stand today? How will we win?* The fourth chapter builds on the discussion of the terror network in chapter one, and deals with the war itself as of early spring 2002. It visits the four crucial countries in the Middle East (Iran, Iraq, Syria, and Saudi Arabia), assesses their internal strengths and weaknesses and their current role in the terror network, and suggests the most effective ways—which vary considerably from one country to another—for us to defeat them.

The "Final Thoughts" and "Looking Forward" sections expand the analysis to some broader reflections on America's role in the world, and provide some basic guidelines with which to evaluate how well our leaders are conducting the war.

1

THE RISE OF THE TERROR NETWORK

When the sacred months are over, slay the idolaters wherever you find them. Arrest them, besiege them and lie in ambush for them.

—KORAN

The murder of man by man is as old as the human race, but the sort of terrorist that attacked the United States on September 11, 2001, is rather new. The concept itself was born during the French Revolution, whose bloodiest phase was known as "The Terror." This led straight to the notion of a "reign of terror," and by the second half of the nineteenth century there were "terrorist" organizations and actors. The most famous of these were Russian, aimed at the overthrow of the czar and the creation of a freer polity, and similar groups came into being all over the world, including anarchists in both the New and Old Worlds, and nationalists and separatists in Central Europe, India, Ireland, and Armenia.

Walter Laqueur, who has long been one of the most astute analysts of terror, credits an obscure German radical democrat, Karl Heinzen, as "the first to produce a full-fledged doctrine of modern terrorism."[1] His magnum opus appeared just one year before the midpoint of the nineteenth century, and laid out the now-familiar strategy of using the mass murder of innocent civilians to achieve political objectives by frightening the rulers into making concessions they would otherwise have rejected. Heinzen even anticipated our contemporary anxiety by praising the destructive power of his day's weapons of mass destruction (bombs, mines, and missiles), and happily predicted great political gains following the murder of 100,000 people in a national capital.

The terrorist movements of the nineteenth century were generally short lived and unsuccessful—often spectacularly so—a pattern that held well into the twentieth century. With the notable exceptions of Zionist terrorism against the British in Palestine (which contributed to the creation of the state of Israel), Palestinian terrorism against Israel, Jordan, Lebanon, and the West (which contributed to the widespread acceptance of the legitimacy of a Palestinian state) and the terrorist campaign of the African National Congress against the apartheid regime in South Africa (which contributed to the victory of "one man, one vote" for all races), terrorists usually made things worse for their announced causes. From Che Guevara in Bolivia in the 1960s to the record levels of murder in Turkey in the 1970s and 1980s, the terrorists generally provoked massive repression rather than the advance of their political objectives. The most tragic example of the terrorists' destructive effect was the Uruguayan Tupamaros, a briefly successful terrorist group that utterly ruined an otherwise civilized and prosperous South American country in the 1960s:

> . . . the only result of their campaign was the destruction of freedom in a country which, alone in Latin America, had had an unbroken democratic tradition of many decades and which had been the first Latin American welfare state . . . The Tupamaros' campaign resulted in the emergence of a right-wing military dictatorship; in destroying the democratic system, they also destroyed their own movement. By the 1970s they and their sympathizers were reduced to bitter protests in exile against the crimes of a repressive re-

gime which, but for their own action, would not have come into existence.[2]

In like manner, the celebrated terrorists of the 1970s and 1980s—from the Palestine Liberation Organization and its various allies to the German Baader-Meinhof Gang, the Italian Red Brigades, the Irish Republican Army, several Turkish groups and the Spanish ETA in Europe, the Symbionese Liberation Army and the Weathermen in the United States, the Shining Path, Tupamaros, Montaneros, FARC, and others in Latin America—suffered defeat after defeat, even though they had significant support from the Soviet Union and its satellites. The targeted countries fought back, invariably restricting civil liberties, increasing police powers, and expanding surveillance. The citizens of these unfortunate countries generally accepted the loss of freedom as an acceptable price for better security, and the terrorists lost whatever popular support they had once had. Even the Palestinians were defeated in the Lebanese War of 1982, driven into temporary exile in Tunisia, and paradoxically rescued by their Israeli and American archenemies. Nonetheless, terrorism continued to plague the West.

Americans, American airliners, and American allies were prime targets from the very beginning. The first hijacking of an American commercial aircraft was carried out by a Puerto Rican activist in May 1961. He forced the plane to land in Cuba and was granted asylum. Seven years later the U.S. ambassador to Guatemala was assassinated in Guatemala City, and within months our ambassador to Brazil was kidnapped by Marxist terrorists. In March 1973, under direct orders from PLO leader Yasser Arafat, U.S. ambassador to Sudan Cleo Noel and others were assassinated inside the Saudi embassy.

The Iran hostage crisis, which began in November 1979, set a new standard, as U.S. diplomats were held by the Khomeini regime until January 20, 1981. Iranian-backed terrorists kidnapped American military and intelligence officers and religious leaders in Lebanon in the mid-1980s, killing some and blackmailing the American government for the release of others. American military installations and other sites frequented by our military personnel were bombed in Germany (Air Force base in Rammstein in August 1981, a discotheque in West Berlin in April 1986), Lebanon (Marine barracks in Beirut, October 1983), Spain (an Air Force base in Torrejon in April 1984 and a servicemen's bar in Barcelona, December 1987), Greece (a bus outside Athens in April 1987), Italy (a USO club in Naples in April 1988) and Saudi Arabia (a military compound in Riyadh in 1995, and the Khobar Towers military housing facility in June 1996).

The biggest and most vulnerable American targets were diplomats and diplomatic facilities, beginning with the Iranian hostage crisis, in which the U.S. embassy in Tehran was assaulted and occupied. Four years later the American embassy in Beirut was bombed by Iranian-backed suicide terrorists. Sixty-three people were killed (including Robert Ames, the CIA's Middle East director) and over a hundred others were wounded. The U.S. embassy in Lima, Peru, was bombed in January 1990, and Iraqi agents placed bombs at a USIS library and at the ambassador's residence in Manila, Philippines, in January 1991. Two American diplomats were gunned down in Karachi, Pakistan in March 1995, the U.S. embassy in Moscow was hit by a rocket-propelled grenade in September of the same year, and the Athens embassy was hit by a rocket in February 1996. The most devastating attack was the simultaneous terrorist bombings of U.S. embassies in Nairobi, Kenya and Dar es Salaam, Tanzania, in August 1998, in which hundreds of American diplomats and private citizens, local employees, and innocent bystanders were killed. Prior to September 11, this was bin Laden's most effective blow against the United States. In October 2000, the U.S. Navy ship *Cole* was bombed by suicide terrorists in a rubber dinghy. Seventeen sailors were killed and thirty-nine others injured.

American commercial airliners were also attacked, most notably the bombing of TWA Flight 840 on final approach into Athens Airport in March 1986, and the total destruction of Pan Am 103 over Lockerbie, Scotland, in December 1988, which killed all 259 persons on board. In early 2001, a Libyan terrorist was convicted of the act.

Americans were also attacked on the seas, as in the *Achille Lauro* hijacking in October 1985 by PLO terrorists. They segregated the Americans from the rest of the passengers, and then murdered an elderly American Jewish paraplegic by pushing him overboard in his wheelchair.

Terrorist attacks on the American homeland were an old story well before September 11. In late January 1975, Puerto Rican separatists bombed Fraunces Tavern in lower Manhattan. Four patrons were killed and another sixty were injured. Two days later, the Weather Underground claimed responsibility for a bomb set off in a bathroom in the State Department. An exiled Chilean diplomat was killed by a car bomb in September 1976 in Washington, D.C. The World Trade Center was bombed by Islamic fundamentalists in February 1993, killing six and wounding a thousand others, and a follow-on plot to bomb the United Nations building and other targets in New York City was foiled shortly thereafter. In February 1997, a Palestinian terrorist shot several tourists on an observation deck of the Empire State Building before killing himself.

American allies were also singled out. Spain, Germany, and Italy were rocked by domestic groups as well as by foreign terrorists, and there were several terrorist bombings in France as well. Great Britain was on a state of constant alert against Irish separatist terrorists, and the prime minister of Sweden was assassinated while walking in Stockholm. Several South Korean ministers and their aides were blown up by North Korean terrorists in Bangkok, and two Indian prime ministers were killed by suicide terrorists.

Terrorism briefly subsided after the fall of the Soviet Empire, because the Soviets had long been the leading sponsors of international terrorism, and the terrorists were significantly weaker without Soviet support. Virtually all the major terrorist organizations, whether in Africa, South America, Western Europe, or the Middle East, received money and weapons directly from Soviet and Central and Eastern European intelligence and military services from the 1960s through the 1980s.[3] These could be and were replaced; the market for weapons is wide open. Money was extorted from vulnerable Middle Eastern governments (particularly those, like Saudi Arabia and the Gulf States, that were extremely wealthy, feeble, and either sympathetic to the terrorists' cause or invitingly weak-willed) and was earned both legally (the great global boom of the nineties was accessible to anyone with some venture capital) and illegally (poppy seeds grow in the Middle East, and drug trafficking produces huge profits). Even without the Soviet Union, the terrorists acquired enough wealth and weaponry to do significant damage.

But a terrorist organization requires more than money and guns. You have to be able to get to your target, and unless you intend to die in the attack you will want an escape route to a safe haven once the operation is over. In practice, logistics and secure facilities were harder to come by than were finances and armaments, and by and large they had come, either directly or indirectly, from the Soviet Empire. The Soviets provided diplomatic "pouches" to secretly move lethal matériel, Soviet intelligence services gave the terrorists false passports and other travel documents of high quality, and Soviet territory was available for military training, indoctrination, and hiding.[4] These indispensable services could not be readily obtained by a handful of terrorists, no matter how skilled and dedicated they might be, and no matter how much money they might have. They could only come from states, of which the USSR was the most important. The radical regimes of Syria, Iran, Iraq, South Yemen, and Libya did the same. After the defeat of the Soviet Empire, the others would have to take up the slack.

Six states provided the vital wherewithal for the Islamic terror network we now combat: Iran, Iraq, Saudi Arabia, Libya, Syria, and Sudan. Of these, Iran was the most important. It was the biggest—sixty million people at the time, now close to seventy million—and the richest, and it had a long national tradition of military skill and strategic deception.

The Iranian Model

Iran is the mother of modern Islamic terrorism. It was part of the fevered vision of the Ayatollah Ruhollah Khomeini, the Shi'ite leader who overthrew the shah in the autumn of 1979. Khomeini was in league with Arab terrorists from the start, forging a military alliance with the PLO and other Palestinian terrorist groups by 1972 at the latest. Thousands of Iranian fighters were trained in the lethal arts by Fatah experts in the PLO's camps in Lebanon, where they also received active assistance from the Syrian regime. Others were trained in camps run by the Popular Front for the Liberation of Palestine inside the tiny Marxist enclave in South Yemen. In that remote hell-hole, Iranians received training from the very best: East German intelligence officers and Cuban terrorist experts.

Before his seizure of power, Khomeini used these terrorists both to attack the shah's regime and to kill off any challengers to his own claim to absolute religious authority. After the revolution of 1979 these skilled killers constituted the hard core of the Pasdaran, the Islamic Revolutionary Guards. The mad vision that we now associate with Osama bin Laden—rage against the desecration of Islamic soil by the presence of unbelievers, the violent expansion of fundamentalist Islam throughout the Middle East, and a global holy war against the infidels outside the Islamic world—was elaborated more than a decade earlier by Khomeini and institutionalized in the Islamic Republic of Iran. Aside from the traditional differences between Sunnis and Shi'ites, bin Laden's doctrines are virtually identical to Khomeini's. Both preach unbridled hatred of America, the Jews, and anything that represents the modern secular state; and both demand the creation of a fundamentalist theocracy throughout the Islamic world. Like Khomeini, bin Laden wants to reestablish the ancient caliphate, where the ruler of the nation was simultaneously the authoritative guide to the faithful.

Khomeini's indictment of the shah was not, as many believe (even including former president Clinton and his secretary of state, Madeleine Albright) that the Iranian government was excessively repressive and intolerant. It was precisely the opposite. According to Khomeini, Iran had become too modern, too tolerant—especially of women and of other religious faiths—and too self-indulgent. The shah had westernized Iran, and in so doing had undermined

11

the power of the mullahs—the religious authorities. The shah had corrupted morality by ending the strict separation of the sexes. He permitted women teachers in boys' schools, and men in girls' schools, "the moral wrongness of which is clear to all."[5] Khomeini raged against the elevation of women to important posts in government and society, and promised to send them to the lower status they were assigned by the faith.[6]

This was only the beginning of Khomeini's indictment of the shah's moral corruption. In the shah's Iran, crimes were judged by lay persons instead of by religious courts. ". . . Jews, Christians, and enemies of Islam and of the Muslims . . . interfere in the affairs of Muslims," and the lay people were far too lenient: "We want a ruler who would cut off the hand of his own son if he steals, and flog and stone his near relative if he fornicates."

Just as bin Laden condemns Saudi Arabia for permitting the presence of infidel American soldiers on her holy land, so Khomeini condemned the shah for his strategic relationship with Israel, which he viewed as a violation of Islamic principles. "What is this . . . association between the shah and Israel . . . is the shah a Jew?" And Khomeini linked Israel and America so intimately that there was virtually no distinction between the two, just as bin Laden does. Israel and America are simply two points of evil along a vast satanic continuum:

It is America which supports Israel and its well-wishers; it is America which gives Israel the power to turn Muslim Arabs into vagrants; it is America which directly or indirectly imposes its agents on the nation of Iran; it is America which considers Islam and the glorious Koran a source of harm to itself and wishes to remove both from its path.

Khomeini was a true revolutionary. No leading Shi'ite had ever called for the overthrow of a legitimate secular leader and his replacement by a religious one. The Shi'ites believe that one of their medieval leaders—the "missing" or Twelfth Imam—will some day return to exercise both religious and political power. Until that messianic day, according to traditional practice, temporal rulers could be tolerated and even supported, so long as they did not try to claim religious power and left the mullahs and ayatollahs free to guide the faithful in the ways of Allah. Khomeini was the first to claim that one man could wield both political and religious power even before the return of the Twelfth Imam.

Moreover, Khomeini was revolutionary in another way: He insisted that the time had come for radical Shi'ism to dominate Islam everywhere. He proclaimed that, since his vision of Islam was the only true version, all Muslims should follow it. He foresaw the restoration of Muhammed's empire under Shi'ite

13

leadership. First Iran, then the rest of the Islamic world. Shi'ites had long been a minority of the Islamic faithful—the Sunnis were many times more numerous—but once the Islamic Republic was established, it would become the inspiration for all believers, transcending all national boundaries. This last was quite in keeping with Muslim tradition, which viewed the community of believers—the "Muslim Nation"—as the fundamental unit. National boundaries were simply lines on a map.

Like bin Laden, Khomeini was an utterly ruthless man, yet pragmatic to the point of cynicism. He might intone against those who disagreed with his theology, and he did not hesitate to have discordant mullahs and ayatollahs assassinated, but he blithely allied himself with anyone who could advance his cause: from Sunni terrorists like Arafat to Marxist unbelievers like the leaders of the PFLP, and even deviants from Islamic tradition like Hafez al-Assad. This last was a member of the Alawites, a small sect of roughly two million that Fouad Ajami terms "the bearers of an esoteric faith which Muslims, both Sunni and Shi'ite, put beyond the pale of Islam."[7] Assad thus came from a tiny minority within a vast sea of Sunnis, and although he was not a particularly observant Muslim, his family background automatically provoked suspicion and enmity. So did his politics, which were secular to the core. His constitution for Syria did not require the leader to be a Muslim and the oath of office of his Ba'ath Party did not mention Allah even once. Many Syrians—both Sunni and Shi'ite—accused Assad of the shah's great crime of having abandoned Islam in favor of secular values.

Khomeini came to Assad's rescue by ordering the imam Moussa Sadr, a celebrated Shi'ite holy man, to support the Ba'ath regime and the Alawites by proclaiming the Alawites legitimate members of the Shi'ite faith. The same was done by the Shi'ite mufti of Tripoli, another Khomeini confederate, Ali Mansur. This vigorous support legitimized Assad in the eyes of many Muslims and helped to stabilize his dictatorship. Assad returned the favor by helping Khomeini train his terrorists in Lebanon, and by giving Khomeini's friends and allies Syrian passports to avoid surveillance and capture by the Iranian intelligence service.

As Martin Kramer neatly summed it up, "Hafez al-Assad needed quick religious legitimacy; the Shi'ites of Lebanon . . . needed a powerful patron. Interests busily converged from every direction."[8] And those converging interests were quite durable; once in power, Khomeini created one of the most dangerous international terrorist groups—Hizbollah— and Assad supported it with many of the same favors.

The ease with which Khomeini formed opportunistic alliances shows something of enormous importance: that even the most fanatical believers may be capable of startling tactical flexibility. Any means are suitable in pursuit of a holy cause, and even the strictest rules of Islamic law can be suspended when circumstances require. One of today's most misleading conventional generalizations about the Islamic world is the suggestion that members of different sects or traditions cannot work together in a common enterprise. It has often been said—even by experienced senior analysts in the American government who should know better—that Sunni and Shi'ite are so profoundly divided that no knowledgeable person could believe that Al Qaeda unites both under a common umbrella. But Al Qaeda does, just as Khomeini did. David Wurmser has provided a clear-eyed picture of the terrorist super-network that operates through Al Qaeda:

> For Syria, the . . . network had the virtue of absorbing and channeling Sunni fundamentalist fervor. Energies that might have been turned against the regime were directed instead against American targets and into Saudi politics. Within the terror network, Shi'ite and Sunni—who otherwise would never have countenanced working together—could join forces, as could secular Palestinians and Islamic extremists . . .

For Iraq, the network offered a way to defeat America. It would be a grave mistake to imagine that Saddam's animus against Saudi Arabia or his secular disposition would prevent him from working with the Wahhabi religious establishment. . . . Sure enough . . . Saddam's regime has lately encouraged the rise, in Iraq's northern safe haven, of Salafism, a puritanical sect tied to Wahhabism that hitherto had been alien to Iraq . . . one of these Salafi movements . . . turns out to be a front for bin Laden.[9]

Furthermore, fundamentalist Muslims like Khomeini and bin Laden have a distinctly modern side to them, despite their well-known hatred of the corruption and sinfulness of the modern world. They may be archreactionaries, but they embrace and master advanced technology when it serves their purposes. Khomeini flooded Iran with audio cassettes of his revolutionary sermons, a brilliant technique of mass manipulation that caught the shah's regime by surprise. Bin Laden's skilled use of satellite phones, videotapes, and the Internet is of a piece with Khomeini's exploitation of the best available Western technology in the 1970s. While it may seem in conflict with his calls to impose medieval religious law on modern societies, the high-tech side of Osama bin

17

Laden is part of the Khomeini model. Had you gone to the short-lived Al Qaeda website[10] you would have found poems by bin Laden, and a competent bit of strategic analysis written by one of bin Laden's top advisers entitled "Fourth-Generation Wars," citing articles by American military and academic counterterrorist authorities.

The willingness of the most radical Islamic fundamentalists to employ the most advanced technology from the infidel West fits neatly with the traditional Islamic division of the world into two parts: the realm of the believers and that of the infidels. Religious rules can be waived for the faithful fighting in the infidels' countries if it is necessary to further the mission of converting, dominating or killing the enemies of Islam. So, for example, some of the September 11 terrorists apparently frequented strip clubs and bars in their Florida neighborhood, which prompted some to suggest they were not "good Muslims." But this was entirely acceptable. It was a tactical deception that was designed to deceive us about their true identities, and thereby contribute to the success of their jihad. It is not only permitted, it's profoundly satisfying to hoist your enemy by his own petard.

The division of the world into believers and unbelievers, the sacred and the profane, is fundamental to Islam and will, in the minds of the believers, last to the end of time:

When the trumpet of the Last Judgment sounds, the dead all rise from their graves and rush to the Field of Judgment "like men rallying to a Standard." There they take up their station before God, in two mighty crowds separated from each other, the faithful on one side and the unbelieving on the other; and each individual is judged by God.[11]

The world itself, and all mankind, are divided into the sacred and the profane, the believers and the infidels. The believers are commanded to impose Islam on the unbelievers, and both the division and the conflict are permanent, at least in this world. ". . . The faithful and the unbelieving are fated to be separate forever and to fight each other. The War of Religion is a sacred duty . . ."

Elias Canetti, one of the great thinkers of the last century, defined Islam as a "religion of war," and while that does not mean that all Muslims feel obliged to wage war against all unbelievers, it is certainly a very strong leitmotif running through Muslim theology. Just before the historic Rabin-Arafat handshake at the White House, one of President Clinton's speechwriters telephoned the greatest Western expert on Islam, Professor Bernard Lewis of Princeton. Could Professor Lewis kindly provide a good quotation from the Koran praising peace and the peacemakers? Professor Lewis promptly obliged.

"Oh, no, we can't use that one," the speechwriter explained. "We already used that quotation the last time. We need a different one." Alas, said Lewis, that was the only such quote he knew of in the entire Koran.

Khomeini's version of Islam was unquestionably bloodthirsty, and both he and his followers spoke of it constantly. He even created a "fountain of blood" in central Tehran, where red water, symbolizing the blood of martyrs who fell in the struggle against the shah and the war with Iraq, cascaded into the pool below. Here, again, Khomeini was a trailblazer, for Iranian terrorist groups—notably Hizbollah and Is-lamic Jihad—raised the recruitment and training of suicide attackers to assembly-line proportions.

As Iraq invaded Iran shortly after the revolution, the early years of the Khomeini regime produced hundreds of thousands of fatalities on the battlefield, and a cult of martyrdom developed in order to enlist young men who would very likely be killed in short order. Stories circulated throughout Iran according to which new recruits were sent into battle without weapons, assured that by the time they came under fire there would be an abundance of available guns in the clutches of their dead predecessors. Few vol-unteer for such experiences without either compulsion or substantial reward, and all the martyrs-to-be were promised instant transfer to paradise, with its legendary pleasures—including the seventy-two dark-eyed perpetual virgins, waiting for you—for all eternity.

The cult of martyrdom permeated Iran's religious institutions, where young Muslims came from throughout the Islamic world to study. Most of them arrived with a high quotient of revolutionary zeal and were easy prey for mullahs working with the intelligence services. Ever the masters of deception, the Iranians took care to select foreigners, and they preferred young men from Sunni countries like Saudi Arabia, Egypt, Algeria, and Tunisia. Tens of thousands of terrorists,[12] including members of Al Qaeda, came out of the seminaries of Qom, Tabriz, and Isfahan. Besotted with their faith and fully prepared to give their lives in a holy struggle against Islam's enemies, these young men were sent to training camps where instructors from as far away as North Korea and Yugoslavia taught them the martial arts. There were special courses in throat slitting and killing with small blades, including carpet or cardboard cutters of the sort used by the September 11 terrorists, a highly prized form of killing because it is both silent and satisfying. These techniques were part of a special course for Arabic-speaking recruits. Some of the graduates became part of elite assassination squads (for example, the killers of former prime minister Shahpour Bakhtiar in Paris), others simply enlisted in the ranks of the terrorist armies, but all were thoroughly prepared, both physically and psychologically.

The same assembly line—from local mosque to theological school to terrorist training camp—functions today on a global scale. The radical mosques and theological schools are no longer limited to Iran and are not even predominantly Shi'ite (most are Wahhabi, which is to say Saudi). They stretch from the Middle East across Europe and the Atlantic to New York, Detroit, and California, across the Pacific to Indonesia, the Philippines, and Singapore into the western hinterland of the People's Republic of China, and finally across Central Asia back to the source. The mosques distribute recruiting materials—both printed and electronic—to the faithful, looking for those with a craving for infidel blood. A video cassette used for this purpose in England was recently described in the London *Observer*: "One video called 'The Mirror of the Jihad' showed Taliban forces in Afghanistan decapitating Northern Alliance soldiers with knives. It was distributed by an Islamic organization based in Paddington, London." Other such materials were found at the Finnsbury Park Mosque in north London, where Zacarias Moussaoui, the accused "twentieth hijacker" of September 11, and

Richard Reid, the accused "sneaker bomber," once prayed.

Look at it as a triumph of globalization: Khomeini was the Henry Ford of Islamic terrorism. He invented the manufacturing technology, and the assembly line was copied everywhere. By the second generation, groups like Al Qaeda found they could recruit with brochures and videos, and then do at least some degree of paramilitary training with user-friendly manuals. They even produced encyclopedias, of the sort captured from Al Qaeda fighters in Afghanistan by the Northern Alliance a couple of years before we enlisted them in the war against terror. It was called *The Encyclopedia of the Afghan Jihad*, and ran to thousands of pages, beginning with a volume on "Explosives," and continuing on through "Weapons" and the other nuts and bolts of the terrorist profession.

The *Encyclopedia of the Afghan Jihad* came in various forms, from abridged books to full-length CD-ROMs, and all were circulated widely. It may not have contained the most advanced lethal technology, but it was good enough for their purposes:

> My expert did not want to be in the kitchen when someone tried to make homemade nitroglycerin per the *Explosives* instructions. But if the process didn't kill its maker, the

resulting ingredients would certainly ex-
plode with great force . . . [13]

Terrorism is a labor-intensive business. But with
an unending supply of cheap manpower, the terror
masters didn't have to worry excessively about occasional accidents. But there was a hidden message
in the very existence of the *Encyclopedia*. Al Qaeda
was not content to limit itself to those people they
could personally recruit and train, one by one; they
were aiming to create a mass movement. They were
trying to inspire Muslims everywhere to take up the
cause of jihad, make their own weapons, and kill all
infidels, including us.

> The *Encyclopedia* was attempting to dimin-
> ish, if not eliminate, the master–pupil tute-
> lage that forced terrorists and would-be
> terrorists to gather together in one spot for
> prolonged study. The volumes were a port-
> able university for the common militant. Its
> ultimate aim was to democratize terrorism.[14]

When the full history of the terror network is
written, we will be surprised at the amazingly large
number of terrorists, and the audacity of their am-
bitions, which frequently exceeded our own. When

talking to Iranian officials in the mid-eighties, I remarked to a high-ranking ayatollah that some day our two countries might get back on good terms. After all, we did share some common interests.

"Absolutely," he snapped back. "Like the Soviet Union. And we are going to bring it down." Few American officials, even during the Reagan years, would have been so outspokenly ambitious. Only later did I discover that Iran was running a substantial operation into Soviet Central Asia, bringing Korans and weapons to the local Muslims so that they could pray and kill communist infidels.

The most potent Iranian-sponsored terrorist organization was, and is, Hizbollah, the Army of God. Americans have suffered at its hands since 1983, when Hizbollah and the PLO combined to blow up the American embassy and then the Marine barracks in Beirut. But this was only the beginning.

- Hizbollah developed a global reach, blowing up the Israeli embassy and then a Jewish community center in Buenos Aires, Argentina, in 1992, killing a hundred civilians, and destroying a Panamanian commuter flight in 1993.

- Hizbollah specialized in kidnaping Westerners in Lebanon, including AP correspondent Terry Anderson, Reverend Benjamin Weir, David Jacobsen, Father Lawrence Jenco, CNN correspondent Charles Glass, journalist Jeremy Levin, British journalist David Hurst, French correspondent Jean-Marc Sroussi, Anglican Church envoy Terry Waite, CIA Beirut station chief William Buckley, American lieutenant colonel William Higgins, several Israeli soldiers and civilians, and many others.

- Hizbollah organized and led the military campaign against Israel in southern Lebanon throughout the 1990s, ending with the Israeli withdrawal.

Khomeini was the spiritual model for Al Qaeda, and Hizbollah, under constant Iranian guidance, provided the organizational model. Both are organized along paramilitary lines, with a governing Shura, or council, headed by the supreme leader (in Hizbollah's case, Sheikh Hassan Nasrallah). Today Hizbollah has operational centers all over the world, including the United States and Canada, South America, Indonesia, Malaysia, France, Germany, England, and Belgium.

Syria controls the Lebanese territory where Hizbollah trains and hides and holds hostages, while Iran commands Hizbollah's top leaders. Whenever key decisions have to be made, either the terrorists go to

Tehran for guidance, or Iranian officials travel to Lebanon. When Hizbollah takes a particularly interesting hostage, experts from Iranian intelligence organizations come to Lebanon to conduct the interrogations. And, although both Syria and Saudi Arabia are also major contributors, Iran keeps tight control over funding.

As in any successful underground organization, Hizbollah leaders understand that effective operations require mass support. The terrorist fish need a popular sea in which to swim, and Hizbollah wins popular support because it is also a social welfare organization, providing health care, food, education, and alms to its followers, in addition to full banking and other financial services. Indeed, a significant part of Hizbollah is now public; Hizbollah members sit in the Lebanese Parliament, having been duly elected by their supporters.

But no matter how generous the social services, or how talented the leadership, you cannot recruit tens of thousands of terrorists without a cause, an inspirational vision. Some would have us believe that terrorist organizations are no more than dangerous cults, that the terrorists are terrorists because they are mentally disturbed, and that if they weren't terrorists they would be suicide cultists like those in Heaven's Gate or Jonestown.[15] There is undoubtedly some truth to the claim that cults attract a certain kind of deranged personality, but in the case of an Islamic fundamentalism, potential recruits are first spotted, then indoctrinated, so that their personalities develop along these lines. And no matter how fervently we would wish it otherwise, these terrorist fundamentalists are Muslims. Their fanatical desire to destroy the West grows out of a deep-seated Muslim rage, and is buttressed by a powerful Muslim doctrine. Without the rage and the doctrine—the ideology of the terror masters—there might be Islamic terrorists (there have been for centuries) but there would not be a global Islamic terrorist network, resting on an Islamic fundamentalist mass movement.

The Crisis of Islam

Like most Muslim thinkers, Osama bin Laden pays great attention to history, and the history of the past fifteen years pleases him enormously. As he reads the recent past, Muslims have racked up a string of impressive victories against some very powerful infidel countries: the Soviet Union, Israel, and the United States. One of his associates fondly went over the list of recent successes:

> In Afghanistan, the Mujahideen triumphed over the world's second most qualitative

power at that time . . . a single Somali tribe humiliated America and compelled it to remove its forces . . . the Chechen Mujahideen humiliated and defeated the Russian bear . . . the Lebanese resistance expelled the Zionist army from southern Lebanon . . . [16]

No matter that the Mujahideen only began to win the war against the Soviet occupation forces when they received weapons—above all, Stinger antiaircraft missiles—money and tactical guidance from the United States, via Pakistan and Saudi Arabia. No matter, either, that the humiliation of a number of American soldiers at Mogadishu was hardly a glorious Islamic victory. Clinton simply decided he couldn't tolerate the spectacle of body bags and dead Americans on the evening news. The "defeat" of the Russian bear in Chechnya was short lived, and Israel withdrew voluntarily from Lebanon.

Radical Islamic fundamentalists overlook these details in favor of an heroic legend of a suddenly resurgent Islam, in bin Laden's words of an Islamic nation that was repeatedly victorious in a way not known since the rise of the Ottoman Empire. In the eyes of bin Laden and other Muslim fundamentalists, this sequence of glorious victories bespeaks a most welcome change in the course of history.

Nothing could be more encouraging to any

thoughtful Muslim than a reversal of the catastrophic trends of the past two or three centuries. For many centuries Muslim civilization was the greatest in the world. The Muslims preserved much of ancient Greek culture at a time when Western Europe had fallen into a continental catatonia that historians have called the Dark Ages. The Muslims far outclassed the Christians in most every area of human endeavor. They were more powerful, more educated, more artistic, more scientific than their Christian rivals. And they were more tolerant and humane. It was far better for minorities like the Jews to live under Muslim rule than under Christian hegemony.

Muslims took these accomplishments as their due, believing as they did that God's words to Mohammed, as recounted in the Koran, constituted the third, final, and only complete revelation of God to man. In their eyes, the manifest superiority of the Muslim world was a Divine reward for their belief in God's revelation to Mohammed. God was on their side, and He gave them glory.

All glorious and inspiring when things go well, but how do you explain centuries of decline, corruption, misery, and humiliation?[17] Have you brought it on yourself? Is Allah punishing you for your sins? If so, is it necessary to reform your ways? Or, perhaps, is it someone else's fault?

The latter explanation is far more psychologically

attractive than the former, and predictably it has been offered more frequently. Arabs have blamed the Turks for the ruin of Islamic civilization, and the Turks have blamed the Arabs. Persians have blamed both Turks and Arabs, and all have blamed foreign colonialists and imperialists, most recently the United States, for stealing Muslim wealth and repressing Muslim genius. Anti-Semitism caught on in the twentieth century, first under Nazi inspiration and then in response to the creation of the Jewish state in Israel. All these themes linger on, even when radical Muslims like Khomeini and bin Laden distribute the blame on the Islamic Nation itself. Islamic rulers are typically condemned for their supine surrender to the infidels. Islamic weakness is blamed on the betrayal of the true faith by Muslim leaders, and a return to fundamentals is presented as the only cure. The indictment is reminiscent of Martin Luther's condemnation of the Catholic Church at the beginning of the Reformation, and of the jeremiads of the Jewish prophets following the destructions of the Temple in Jerusalem, and the long exile in the Diaspora. It

attributes all evil to the abandonment of the divine heritage of Islam and advocates return to a real or imagined past. That is the way of the Iranian revolution and of the so-

called fundamentalist movements and regimes in various countries.[18]

Allah consigned the Muslims to decline and humiliation because they forgot His revelation, strayed
from His ways, and adopted the ways of the infidels.
Muslims will become strong when they return to the
ancient truths.

That is why Osama bin Laden's close reading of
recent events is so important, for he is able to argue
that the only Muslims who can defeat infidels are
those who derive their strength from Allah. Unlike
the losers throughout the Muslim world—who are
dominated by infidel culture, infidel technology, and
infidel armies—they have rejected the corruption of
the modern Arab states and embraced the true faith,
just as it was when Muslims ruled the civilized world.
It's a powerful message, for it "explains" the world to
those disinclined to look unflinchingly at history, and
it gives meaning to the lives of those who embrace it.

In 1990, before anyone outside the Middle East
had heard of bin Laden, Bernard Lewis warned the
West that we were in for a very tough time. "It
should now be clear," he wrote, "that we are facing a
mood and a movement far transcending the level of
issues and policies and the governments that pursue
them." We faced what Lewis elegantly termed "the
perhaps irrational but surely historic reaction of an

ancient rival against our Judeo-Christian heritage, our secular present, and the worldwide expansion of both."[19]

Osama

Like Khomeini, Osama bin Laden assembled a terrorist coalition to wage jihad against the West in the name of fundamentalist Islam. There were two main differences between them, aside from the formal conflicts between Sunni and Shi'ite doctrines. Khomeini ruled a country, while Osama needed state support to become a potent force. Also, Osama was not a theological innovator, while Khomeini was a theological revolutionary. Osama did not need to be an innovator, for the official doctrine of his native Saudi Arabia was the Sunni equivalent of Khomeini's version of Shi'ism.

The Saud family conquered Arabia in the early twentieth century in no small measure because of the support of the Wahhabis, a violent, puritanical fundamentalist Sunni sect named after its founder, Ibn Abdul Wahhab (1703–1792).

Wahhabism is the Islamic equivalent of the most extreme Protestant sectarianism. It is puritan, demanding punishment for those who enjoy any music except the drum, and severe punishment . . . for drinking or sexual transgressions.

It [calls for] simple, short prayers, undecorated mosques, and the uprooting of gravestones (since decorated mosques and graveyards lend themselves to veneration, which is idolatry in the Wahhabi mind). Wahhabis do not even permit the name of the Prophet Mohammed to be inscribed in mosques, nor do they allow his birthday to be celebrated. Above all, they hate ostentatious spirituality, much as Protestants detest the veneration of miracles and saints in the Catholic Church.[20]

The Wahhabis' rejection of anything that portrayed the human figure has often been carried to extremes, as it was in 2001, when the Taliban dynamited two enormous stone statues of Buddha in Afghanistan. Once again, there is an Iranian parallel: After the revolution, Khomeini forbade the production of carpets that carried the images of living things. Henceforth only geometrical and floral designs were permitted. In addition, despite their celebration of certain aspects of Muslim history, the Wahhabis can be quite contemptuous of relics of the Muslim past. In January 2002, the Saudis demolished the two-hundred-year-old (Ottoman) al-Ayed Castle in central Mecca, to make room for a parking lot. Turkey's cultural minister protested with UNESCO, denounced the Saudi "crime against humanity," and noted that there was no difference between the Taliban action the year before—which had been denounced by the global intelligentsia—and the destruction of "this legacy of the Ottoman era."[21]

The Wahhabis venerated and practiced violence on a grand scale, and were credited for several famous massacres during the nineteenth and twentieth centuries. Their support was crucial in the military victories of the Saud family in the 1920s, and King ibn Saud rewarded them by making Wahhabism the official faith of the Saudi state.

Osama imbibed Islamic fundamentalism because it was part of growing up in Saudi Arabia. It was the message of his mosque and the basic language of Saudi Wahhabi doctrine. He had ample opportunity to spread the faith, for the wherewithal to advance his crazed vision came with his birth certificate. His father Muhammed created one of the kingdom's leading business conglomerates (the Bin Laden Group), and he maintained his more than fifty children in great luxury, but Osama was fully prepared to leave his gilded world in order to fight infidels. The call to arms came when the Soviet Union invaded Afghanistan at the end of 1979. "I was enraged and went there at once," Osama said, "I arrived within days."

He would like us to believe otherwise, but Osama

was not a great fighter in Afghanistan. He worked on finance and logistics, the precursor of his terror network. Over the next nine years he contributed many family millions to the Mujahideen fighters, raised additional funds throughout the Gulf, and created Al Qaeda, originally a charitable organization that expanded its philanthropic work worldwide, including an office in the United States, to fund extremist groups. In the course of his work he created recruitment centers and guest houses in Egypt, Pakistan, and Saudi Arabia that gave sustenance to thousands of volunteer fighters and workers; created paramilitary training camps for his recruits in Pakistan, Sudan, and Afghanistan; and brought heavy landmoving equipment to Afghanistan in order to create a network of roads and tunnels. (American armed forces subsequently attacked pieces of this network during the Afghan campaign in 2001–2002). He was also deeply involved in financing radical Islamic groups that carried the struggle to moderate Arab governments.

It has often been said that bin Laden is a classic example of "blowback," that is, an operation aimed against an enemy that rebounds against the attackers. According to this view, the United States supported radical Islamic forces against the Red Army in Afghanistan and now finds itself at war with many of those same Islamic radicals, with bin Laden in the front rank. It's the Middle Eastern version of Frankenstein's monster. There is some truth to the accusation, but not much. In the late eighties and early nineties there were precious few Americans on the ground in Pakistan, let alone Afghanistan, where virtually no one from the Pentagon or the CIA was permitted to operate. The Islamic forces were mostly funded by the Saudis and mostly trained by the Pakistanis. The really telling American failure in Afghanistan was not an excess of zeal but a lack of engagement and follow-through. If we had been more fully involved in the war against the Soviets in Afghanistan, we might have taken steps to dismantle the Mujahideen networks, or penetrate them, or at least remove the most dangerous weapons, like Stinger missiles. This never happened.

If there was any blowback from Afghanistan, it blew back against the Saudis and the Pakistanis, and only indirectly against us. When bin Laden returned to his native land after the great victory against the Soviets, he found American troops on Saudi soil, and this drove him into a famous rage. He denounced the monarchy for permitting "crusaders and Jews" to despoil the sacred land of the prophet, and pronounced Saudi leaders unworthy of their holy mission. This has remained one of his central themes, prompting many serious analysts to conclude that bin Laden aims at conquering his own country.

He and Al Qaeda are certainly incomprehensible without understanding their intimate connection to Saudi religious doctrines and an ongoing power struggle within the kingdom. "At its core, Al Qaeda is a product of Saudi dynastic politics," Wurmser tells us. Its purpose is "to swing Saudi politics toward the Wahhabi establishment . . . but not necessarily to destroy the royal family, at least not at first . . ."[22]

In keeping with our past overseas behavior, we simply lost interest once the main enemy, the Soviet Union, was defeated. Americans do not believe that conflict is normal, so once the war was over we went back to "normal." This traditional compulsion was reinforced by the subsequent collapse of the Soviet Union itself, at which point we temporarily stopped worrying about the entire region, save for the "peace process" involving Israel and the Palestinians.

Plus, there was a form of cultural arrogance: Arabs' warrior virtues are not highly respected in Western capitals. The stereotype of the Arab does not include qualities that induce fear and respect. Aside from a handful of counterterrorism experts, very few policy makers were inclined to think deeply about what the Afghan Arabs would do after they left Afghanistan. After all, they had been cannon fodder for the Red Army before we arranged to have them properly trained and armed; why should we be concerned? So Osama and his cohorts had a free ride.

The American government wasn't worried, and wasn't going to pay much attention. This was another recurring blunder, since U.S. policy makers had already made the same mistake concerning the Iranians. The United States had trained Iran's military and intelligence elite during the shah's rule, but once Khomeini came to power the Iranian image in Washington changed drastically. Instead of the most advanced Islamic country, Iran was taken to be just another Third-World dictatorship, perhaps a bit crazier than most, but surely no serious threat to the United States.

Our leaders should have remembered the joke about the man who has a flat tire in front of an insane asylum. He jacks up the car, removes the flat, and carefully puts the lugs in the hubcap, at which point a motorcycle speeds past, clips the edge of the hubcap, and sends the lugs flying down a drain. The man stands helplessly, wondering what to do, when an inmate on the other side of the asylum fence says, "It's not so bad. You've got three more tires with four lugs per tire. Three are plenty to hold the wheel in place. Just take one lug from each of the other wheels and put on the spare, and then buy yourself four new lugs later on, one for each wheel."

The man does as he is told, and as he is getting ready to drive off he asks the inmate if he lives in the asylum. "Yes."

"Well, then, how were you able to solve that problem so easily?"

"Hey," says the inmate, "I may be crazy, but I'm not stupid."

Fanatics can be powerfully pragmatic and effective, and they can act with a single-mindedness that eludes more balanced personalities. American policy makers finally got that message on September 11.

The Soviets withdrew from Afghanistan in 1989, and bin Laden returned to his family's construction business in Saudi Arabia the following year, still maintaining his close working relations with radical Islamic groups that targeted moderate Arab governments. Even worse, he openly denounced the royal family for permitting American troops to use Saudi bases during the Gulf War. The Saudi government *was* concerned, and they showed it by withholding his passport for nearly two years to prevent him from meeting overseas with extremists. Given the close working relationship between Saudi intelligence and the CIA, our people would have started to track Osama at that time.

He got his passport back at the end of 1991, and early the next year bin Laden moved to Khartoum, where he combined work for the family business (building a major highway and an airport) with his expanding terrorist activities. This is one of the many features of his career that led people to think of bin Laden as the CEO of a multinational terrorist corporation; he has been very imaginative at finding ways to make money from his terrorist ventures. The most spectacular of these—if indeed it happened—was playing the European stock market to take advantage of the terrorist attacks he'd ordered for September 11. He is said to have shorted the shares of the insurance companies covering the World Trade Center. If it's not true, it's still a great tale, as the Italians say, and it properly draws our attention to the considerable sophistication of Al Qaeda. They may be crazy, but they're demonstrably not stupid.

Sudan had fallen under the sway of a Wahhabi-style regime, and bin Laden was a most welcome guest. Over the next five years, he financed terrorists throughout the region, worked with the Sudanese government to create a series of terrorist training camps in the northern part of the country, and extended his reach to the likes of Ramsey Yousef, the architect of the first World Trade Center bombing. In this period he funded attacks against American military personnel on a peacekeeping mission in Aden, designed and financed terrorist attacks against Egypt in concert with the Egyptian Jihad group, and provided training to thousands of terrorists from Egypt, Algeria, Tunisia, and Yemen.

It was not all scheming and safe havens, however.

Osama wanted to join the fight against the unbelievers in Southern Sudan, and he was furious when the Sudanese government wouldn't let him play. And he had to pay a price for his years in Sudan: The government took hefty commissions from his business activities, and wasn't always convinced that Al Qaeda was paying its full dues.

Looking at bin Laden's activities in Sudan, one is struck by his support for Egyptian terrorists; Egypt is a country that does not often figure in his diatribes. The attention to Egypt was probably not his originally, but his sponsors', for there was constant tension between Egypt and Sudan in those years. When bin Laden started to operate in the region, it should have set off multiple alarm bells in Washington. Egypt is the biggest single recipient of American aid, and it would not serve our interests to have the government of Egypt fall to Islamic fundamentalists. Moreover, a partnership between Al Qaeda and the Egyptian Islamic Jihad was a serious matter. The Egyptian Jihad was responsible for the assassination of Anwar Sadat, and was a potent force. If you added Al Qaeda's wealth and organizational skills to the Jihad's murderous manpower, you got a major threat. They started working together in Sudan, and the merger was complete no later than 1998. And that threat became even more sinister with the addition of Hizbollah and the Palestinians.

Sudan in the early nineties expanded what had been created in Lebanon a decade earlier: a meeting-place for the terror network, a training ground for their troops, a haven for their intelligence officers, and a place where the various groups and leaders could exchange information, ideas, and war stories. People who lived in Khartoum in those years tell of a colorful parade of foreign visitors, from countries as diverse as Egypt, Iran, Iraq, Syria, China, Cuba, Indonesia, and the Philippines, the states of the Caucuses from Georgia to Central Asia, and the north African trio of Libya, Tunisia, and Algeria. Both Iran and Iraq established significant intelligence head-quarters in Khartoum, and both had contacts with bin Laden, as did the Syrians and the leaders of the main terrorist groups, from Hizbollah on down. They all envied and hated America, welcomed bin Laden's campaign against "moderate" Arab regimes, and were engaged in the same sort of terrorist operations as Al Qaeda. Future events confirmed the intimacy of their relationships.

By the mid-nineties bin Laden had acquired a significant international profile. The Saudis revoked his passport in 1994, and his oldest brother, Bakr, con-temporaneously announced the family's "regret, de-nunciation, and condemnation" of Osama's behavior. As mentioned earlier, the State Department an-nounced in 1996 that bin Laden was the greatest single financier of terrorist projects in the world. Even though he hadn't killed very many infidels, his organizational talents had not gone unnoticed.

The first American effort to disrupt Al Qaeda's operations came in the same year—1996—when the Clinton administration encouraged the Sudanese government to expel bin Laden, thereby forcing his relocation to Afghanistan. It was not a great success for American counterterrorism; Al Qaeda quickly built a new network of terrorist training camps in Afghanistan. Worse still, the Taliban regime proved even more supportive than the Sudanese, and it's fair to say that Afghanistan under Mullah Omar was the world's second radical Islamic terrorist state (after Khomeini's Iran). His home base secured, bin Laden sent additional troops to train in the traditional places: Iraq, Syria, and Lebanon's Bekka Valley, the long-standing Iran/Syria joint venture.

Thanks to court testimony from persons involved in the 1998 bombings of the American embassies in Kenya and Tanzania, we know a good deal about Al Qaeda's internal structure. We know there is a governing council called the Shura, which controls various other councils that manage the military, financial, communications, and intelligence needs of the group. In short, it's a national security apparatus under the overall command of Osama. So long as he was based in Afghanistan, there was a convenient overlap between Al Qaeda and the Taliban state. But once the Taliban was destroyed, bin Laden needed increased assistance from the other state sponsors.

The Nature of the Terror Network

Western intelligence services have long been reluctant to accept the fact that modern Islamic terrorism is above all else a weapon used by hostile nation states against their enemies in the Middle East and in the West. Although testimony from Director of Central Intelligence George Tenet has moved steadily toward accepting a far greater degree of organization, the CIA long maintained that even an organization as well structured as Al Qaeda is a "loose association" of terrorist groups, a definition that is crafted with a political intent. First of all, it suggests a certain spontaneity to the elements of the terror network, avoiding any implication of control or decisive influence, either from a state or from a terror master like bin Laden. As late as the end of 2001, the CIA insisted that while the various groups and even national intelligence services may have cooperated in some operations, they did not constitute a well-organized terrorist network.

The intelligence community fought against the notion of a coherent terror network throughout 2001, demonstrating once again how abysmal our intelligence continued to be. On the last day of the year, James Risen of *The New York Times* reported on classified American documents showing that there had been contacts between Al Qaeda and Iranian intelligence officers in 1995 and 1996 (before bin Laden's move to Afghanistan). Risen's article, clearly reflecting the convictions of CIA analysts, noted that "Iran . . . has tended to support Shi'ite-based extremist groups like Hizbollah . . . rather than Sunni Muslim extremists like Al Qaeda."[23]

Yet the same article noted that an American grand jury had indicted thirteen Saudis (heavy favorites to be Sunni) and a Lebanese in the 1996 Khobar Towers bombing. And "the indictment implicated Iranian officials . . ." In other words, radical Shi'as and Sunnis worked together.

We may never know the full story, for when the Saudis found convincing witnesses, they promptly decapitated them before any American could interrogate them. Probably the Saudis, too, were afraid of the consequences if they permitted the witnesses to identify the Iranian terror masters. As Risen wrote, "the Bush Administration, like the Clinton Administration before it, has been eager to improve relations with Iran and has not talked of it as a possible target in President Bush's new global campaign against terror." It would be hard to have improved relations with a country that was actively killing your own citizens.

The unwillingness to recognize that Iran and Al Qaeda were working together prevented us from understanding the nature of the terror network, and blinded us to what was actually going on on the ground in Afghanistan. The best way to think of the terror network is as a collection of mafia families. Sometimes they cooperate, sometimes they argue, sometimes they even kill one another. But they can always put aside their differences whenever there is a common enemy. As in *The Godfather*, sometimes the Barzinis and the Corleones and the others join together to fight the feds. In this case, we're up against all five families, not just one. If they killed us, they'd go back to fighting over turf and methods. But in the meantime, it's all for one and one for all.

If American policy makers had understood this, we might have had better success in capturing Osama bin Laden in Afghanistan. As American forces hunted for him and for other Al Qaeda leaders, American intelligence officers focused their attention on the eastern border with Pakistan instead of toward the western border with Iran. When I asked a top analyst at the CIA in December 2001 why we were not more concerned about the possibility that bin Laden would be rescued by the Iranians, I was patiently told that this was highly unlikely since Sunnis and Shi'ites just didn't work together that closely. Yet the CIA soon had dramatic evidence of Sunni–Shi'ite cooperation in the celebrated case of the *Karine A*, the ship loaded with tons of explosives and Iranian weapons intercepted in early 2002 by the Israeli Defense Forces en route from Dubai—a major Iranian operational base—to the Palestinian Authority. Iran is the operational definition of Shi'ism, and the Palestinians are Sunnis.[24] The weapons were Iranian and the ship and its captain were Sunni. If that didn't cause our experts to reconsider the theory of unbridgeable Sunni/Shi'ite hostility, what would?

And how would they explain the intimate cooperation—now a full thirty years of it—between Iranian Shi'ites and Syrian Alawites in Lebanon, where Hizbollah received support and protection from both governments?

By mid-February, 2002, all that had changed. The president was able to see the picture more clearly than many of his Middle East experts. Bush listed Iran as a charter member of the "axis of evil," Secretary of Defense Donald Rumsfeld announced his displeasure with Iranian assistance to escaping Al Qaeda terrorists and surviving Taliban fighters, and Bill Gertz of the Washington *Times* reported that we were aware of "scores" of Iranian military and intelligence officers operating deep inside Afghanistan to destabilize the interim government and drive out

American forces. Having finally gathered firsthand intelligence on the ground in Afghanistan, Pentagon officials spoke openly about Al Qaeda fighters moving into Iran, some of them transiting the country for destinations from the Palestinian Authority to Yemen. Others remained, having found a safe haven in the Islamic Republic. Given all this, no one in the Pentagon was surprised in early May 2002, when Israel sank yet another ship carrying weapons from the Iranian-sponsored Hizbollah to the Palestinians in Gaza.

The U.S. intelligence community, which had scoffed at the very idea of Iran/Al Qaeda cooperation, now seriously considered the possibility that bin Laden himself was hiding in the Islamic Republic. Nobody knew exactly where bin Laden had found refuge, but it would be entirely in character for the Shi'ite tyrants in Tehran to hide him. Their faith revolves around a "vanished imam," and they would understand that bin Laden might become even more powerful if he, too, vanished. The Iranians were adept at creating myths; they would relish turning bin Laden into a legendary figure. "Vanishing" bin Laden inside Iran would be easy, since, in addition to the normal hiding places in a country of seventy million people, there was a vast covert facility: The Chinese and North Koreans had dug an elaborate network of tunnels just north of Tehran, where weapons, ammunition, laboratories, and guests requiring total privacy could be secreted. Bin Laden was used to living in caves and tunnels, after all.

In all probability, the working relationship between Al Qaeda and Iran was forged in the Afghan war against the Soviet Union, and continued uninterrupted throughout the nineties. There were certainly many contacts during Osama's Sudan years, and while his move to Afghanistan and his intimate relationship with the Taliban (an enemy of Iran) undoubtedly caused problems, the link was never broken. Indeed, people in a position to know claim that shortly after September 11, bin Laden sent a video cassette to Tehran, thanking the Iranian leaders for their precious assistance.

Iran's intentions with regard to Afghanistan were crystal clear: Iranian mullahs and ayatollahs wanted to turn Afghanistan into a second Lebanon. In the 1980s the Iranians' fearsome Islamic terrorist organization, Hizbollah, had driven out the Americans by taking hostages and blowing up military and diplomatic facilities, and in the nineties similar methods had driven out the Israelis. The mullahs hoped to use the same methods to achieve the same glorious result in Afghanistan. It was no accident that anti-Israeli terrorism increased dramatically after the defeat of the Taliban; it was part of the counteroffensive by the terror masters.

Just as they did in Lebanon in the eighties and

nineties, all elements in the network cooperate with one another today. After Bush's "axis of evil" speech, Iran, Iraq, and Syria designed contingency plans in the event of an American attack against any one of them, and Iranian officials flew to North Korea for consultations. By mid-March 2002, there were twice-weekly flights of transport planes between Tehran and Iraq, there were regular flights between Iran and Saudi Arabia, and to and from Damascus. Intelligence operatives from Baghdad, Tehran, and Damascus were planning anti-Israeli operations based in Lebanon. On March 9, the London *Daily Telegraph* reported that the United States and Britain had concluded that Iran and Iraq were cooperating closely to rescue Al Qaeda survivors from Afghanistan ("large numbers of Al Qaeda and Taliban fighters were seen in northern Iraq after fleeing Afghanistan"), and that Iran was helping Saddam rearm. Moreover, American and British intelligence sources told the *Telegraph* that Iran and Iraq had "connived . . . to allow Al Qaeda fighters to use Iraqi airspace to fly from Iran to Lebanon after the fall of the Taliban regime . . ."[25]

Al Qaeda had lost its operational base in Afghanistan, but it had quickly acquired a new one in Lebanon and the Palestinian Authority. Bin Laden had lost a battle, but was still engaged in holy war against the West. And he had the full support of the ruling terror masters in the Middle East.

The terror war started in Afghanistan, against bin

Laden and the Taliban. It continued as the most lethal of our enemies—Iran—moved onto the battlefield. Meanwhile, the other terror masters advanced
apace. Saddam Hussein was rebuilding his facilities
to produce weapons of mass destruction, as well as
the missiles he needed to deliver them onto neighboring territory, especially Israel. Power in Syria
passed from Hafez al-Assad to his son Bashar with
no noticeable change in policy; Syria refused to even
discuss the possibility of arresting or expelling the
terrorist groups under her protection, and they continued full cooperation with Iran, Hizbollah, and Al
Qaeda in Lebanon.

And all the while, largely unnoticed by the experts, a network of radical Islamic mosques and
schools was spreading all over the United States, rais-
ing young American Muslims to hate Jews and Christians, and encouraging them to join the terrorist
ranks, even if it meant their own martyrdom.

2

THE HOME FRONT

Bring down their airliners. Prevent the safe passage of their ships. Occupy their embassies. Force the closure of their companies and banks.
  —Fax from Osama bin Laden to his friend and ally, Sheikh Omar Bakri Mohammed, in London.

In the last decade of the Cold War, the United States government discovered that there were "sleeper" networks of Arab terrorists inside the United States. The first was revealed to us, as so many of our enemies' secrets are, by a defector, someone from the other side who decides he belongs with us. The man in question had been a KGB station chief in North Africa in the early 1980s and he brought over a detailed list of the terror sleepers, complete with names, ad-

53

dresses, and even some telephone numbers. For the most part, these individuals—who were members of one of the most extremely violent Palestinian groups—were ideally suited to penetrate American society, take up residence among us, and blend into the background. Unlike the popular stereotype of terrorists as coming from the lowest levels of society (and therefore driven to desperate violence by their misery), these were professionals. They were doctors, lawyers, and teachers, and they knew the English language.

In short, they were very much like the September 11 terrorists, who also came from comfortable backgrounds, were well educated, and easily penetrated our society. Had it not been for the Soviet defector, we would never have noticed them.

Like many defectors, this one was wary of the CIA. One day when he was alone with some FBI debriefers, he pulled some handwritten pages from beneath his shirt, and thrust them into the hands of the nearest FBI agent. They contained his handwritten description of the extensive sleeper network in the United States, along with names, addresses, and telephone numbers of the terrorists-in-waiting. In short order, FBI field offices were instructed to carefully watch all the people on the list, and they did, for many years.

It was an impressive organization. The sleepers

took up residence all over the country in the early and mid-eighties, from the New York suburbs of northern New Jersey to Santa Fe, New Mexico and San Jose, California. They were exceedingly well trained in the techniques of evading surveillance; so good, in fact, that the Bureau found it impossible to trail them on foot or in automobiles, and FBI agents were forced to use aircraft to follow the sleepers' movements in the cities.

The other sleeper network was uncovered by the CIA in 1986. The Counterterrorism Center recruited a member of the Abu Nidal organization, at the time one of the most dangerous Palestinian groups, and the Agency's new agent reported that there would be a meeting of leading international terrorists in the Mediterranean area in the fall of 1986. The CIA monitored the meeting, and then tracked one of the participants—a nondescript Palestinian Arab by the name of Zein al-Abdeen Hassan Isa—back to St. Louis, Missouri. By monitoring Isa's activities and listening to his telephone conversations, the FBI uncovered a substantial number of Abu Nidal operatives, and placed them all under surveillance.

Like the network the KGB defector exposed to us, the Abu Nidal group was also a nationwide organization, with cells in numerous American cities, including Cleveland, Detroit, St. Louis, and San Diego. One of the major branches of the network was in St.

Louis, and several of its members attracted considerable attention from our intelligence community, as well as from the Israeli Mossad, in the spring of 1987, when they flew to Mexico City to meet with the Abu Nidal official in charge of operations in the Americas.[1] He had the now-striking name of Mahmoud Atta (although he was unrelated to the September 11 ringleader of the same name). Atta instructed them to target "Jewish and related American targets for terrorist acts"[2] (Abu Nidal's main mission), to raise money for the movement's global operations, to amass and hide weapons, to recruit new members, and to pay special attention to American counterintelligence, both among the local police and, above all, the FBI. Any member of the community who cooperated with the FBI was to be targeted for execution.

As one of the FBI men on the case remarked, "They're as organized as the Mafia but not nearly as lovable. . . . The Mafia has more respect for human life. The mob only offs members and those who've crossed them. This group is far more violent, far more dangerous. You'll see."[3]

The most important of the St. Louis cell was Zein Isa, the Palestinian who had attended the 1986 terrorist summit. Isa entered the United States through Puerto Rico, where it was easier to slip past U.S. Immigration than at a major mainland airport. In order to appear more "normal," Isa married a local woman before moving on to Missouri.

Zein Isa was a small shopkeeper, but his middling status belied his importance to the terror network, because he was in touch with other shopkeepers all over the country. Together, they conspired to bilk the government by running scams with newspaper coupons and food stamps, as well as the usual lying about income to the IRS. A lot of the money headed back to Mahmoud Atta for terrorist activities in Israel and Western Europe.

Although Zein Isa had a wife and children in the West Bank—something he told his new wife only after their wedding—the second marriage proved durable, and they produced three children. Two of them accepted the stern patriarchy traditional in the Muslim Middle East, but daughter Tina assimilated too successfully and demanded the freedom normally accorded American teenagers. This earned her threats and repeated beatings, which got worse when she began dating a local African-American boy. Isa hated black people, and he could not tolerate Tina's relationship, which he viewed as insulting and humiliating. He concluded that she had gone over to the other side, and was therefore a double risk. Her refusal to break off her romantic relationship proved she did not honor her father, and she might well betray him to American authorities.

On the night of November 3–4, 1989, Tina came home late to find her father waiting for her with a knife. Her mother held her down by the hair while

Isa shouted "Die, my daughter, die!" as he stabbed her over and over again. The terrible scene was recorded on an FBI tape.

Isa predictably insisted to the local police that his daughter was crazy and had attacked him, and that he had been forced to use the knife to defend himself, and for a while Isa's defenders thought they might even get him off. The FBI wasn't enthusiastic about presenting their tape—although they could hardly withhold evidence in a criminal proceeding—because the Abu Nidal sleepers would immediately realize that they were all at risk.

And so it was; from the moment of Zein's arrest on November 7, the well of information from tapped telephone calls and bugged conversations all over the United States went bone dry. Zein was found guilty and locked away for murder, the others in his cell were convicted of relatively minor infractions, and in the meantime Abu Nidal had turned his murderous paranoia against his own people in a destructive frenzy that makes one think of Stalin's purges or the Chinese Cultural Revolution.

There will be more about Abu Nidal's murderous paranoia in the next chapter; for the moment the issue is our awareness of networks of terrorist sleepers in the United States. And the central fact is that we have known of their existence for a long time and we've continued to see more of them crop up. By the mid-1990s the FBI had learned of a third sleeper network, this one run by Hizbollah, the infamous Iranian-backed organization that has killed hundreds of Americans in Lebanon and Saudi Arabia over the past two decades. It's not as if the FBI suddenly discovered the phenomenon on the morning of September 11. Indeed, the FBI's ability to round up hundreds of suspects within a day or two after September 11 must have rested at least in part on information they had gathered by watching the sleepers they knew about. So far as I know, the sleepers didn't act (that's why they're called "sleepers," after all); but they did have contacts, they did raise and transmit money for their organizations, and they had to maintain a certain level of skill and discipline. These activities made them vulnerable to attentive surveillance. Some of them, for example, used to go to the southern California desert for shooting practice, and the FBI bugged a nearby campsite they used for barbecues. Over time, this systematic search for useful information pays off.

It is a commonplace in the literature on intelligence that one's successes remain secret while the failures make the front pages, and it's only fair to say that, even so, we know that our domestic counterterrorism program had a number of successes. Many other happy stories—according to former FBI officials, more than fifty during the 1980s alone, including planned assassinations and other schemes that would have killed thousands of Americans—are still classified, awaiting their chronicler. Some victories were produced by alert Americans and panicky terrorists, like the immigration officer who spotted a truck carrying large quantities of explosives headed south across the U.S.–Canadian border in late 1999, apparently destined for Los Angeles International Airport. Others came from good old-fashioned police work, like the investigation following the World Trade Center bombing in early 1993, which uncovered a further plot to bomb the Lincoln and Holland Tunnels under the Hudson River. Still others came from the happy combination of good fortune and good friends, as when, in 1995, fire broke out in the home of Arab terrorists in the Philippines. This led to the arrest of one terrorist and the discovery of an enormous amount of literature, including plans to simultaneously bomb a dozen American commercial aircraft in flight over the Pacific. It also catalyzed the full realization, at least at the highest levels of the FBI, that the United States was riddled with terrorist cells.

Yet even our successes contained worrisome evidence that we were nowhere near the level of effectiveness that the extensive threat demanded. For example, while our law enforcement teams in New York City quickly rounded up most of the perpetrators of the first World Trade Center bombing, they should have seen it coming. On September 1, 1992, Ramsey Yousef—the leader of the team that bombed the World Trade Center early the following year—flew from Pakistan to New York, along with a man named Ahmed Mohammed Ajaj. They were traveling with stolen European passports, thereby avoiding annoying controls at Immigration, and headed for the customs line. Yousef had only a small carry-on and breezed through, but Ajaj had several big suitcases. For some reason Ajaj was asked to open them, thereby revealing a fascinating collection of terrorist literature (how-to books and videos on bomb-making, suicide attacks, avoiding surveillance— especially at U.S. Customs and Immigration— killing Jews, etc.) and a considerable quantity of false and stolen passports and other travel documents and IDs.

Ajaj was not a major terrorist—indeed, the author of the best book on the World Trade Center plot argues convincingly that his post-bombing life sentence was terribly unfair[4]—but he was traveling with the key conspirator, and the production of false documents is one of the most important elements in terrorist enterprises. Sooner or later, most successful terrorists become known, and can no longer travel safely under their own names. Ajaj's suitcases should have set off alarm bells. Somebody, at some point well before the bomb exploded in downtown Manhattan, should have realized that Ajaj was worth more than what they gave him at first: a mere six months in jail for traveling under a false passport (possession of terrorist literature and guides to breaking laws from import duties to homicide, are all protected by the current interpretation of the First Amendment).

But bureaucrats don't solve problems, they apply the rules. There was no rule that said that Customs and Immigration officials have to pay special attention to an Arab-looking visitor from the Middle East traveling on a Swedish passport, with a suitcase full of phony travel documents and do-it-yourself terror instructions and cassettes. You can't prosecute an individual for his reading and viewing habits in our free country. The only law he broke was traveling on a phony passport. So you get a pat on the back for arresting him on the passport violation, and nobody yells at you for leaving the treasure-trove in his suitcases unreported to those who might know what to do with it. The FBI was not informed, and knew nothing about Ajaj's terrorist kit until after the World Trade Center was bombed in 1993.

This pattern recurs over and over again. The separate organizations designed to maintain domestic security simply do not work with one another. The State Department complains that they're not getting enough reliable intelligence from the CIA and the FBI. The head of the Immigration and Naturalization Service, James Ziglar, protests that the FBI waited many months after the 1993 Trade Center bombing before giving INS access to the very thorough National Crime Information Center databases, and then at only two entry points. State Department officials insist that they could have stopped several of the September 11 terrorists if they'd received better information from the intelligence agencies.[5] And the FBI complains that the CIA keeps them in the dark, as when Malaysian intelligence officers informed the CIA in January 2000 about an Al Qaeda meeting in Kuala Lumpur that included two of the September 11 hijackers. The CIA never followed up, the Malaysian government did not maintain surveillance over the group, and the FBI didn't hear about it until after the September 11 attack.

The complaints are legitimate, but the problems go much deeper. The numbers show that it's not just a matter of networking the various organizations; sometimes they just don't work, period. By early 2002, there was a backlog of more than 50,000 immigration appeals, and 314,000 persons ordered deported were still in the United States. The INS famously informed a Florida flight school in the spring of 2002 that Mohammed Atta's student visa had been issued, and the FAA continued to send the

latest guidelines for pilots to some of the 9/11 terrorists as late as April 2002.

Officials at JFK Airport didn't know that Ajaj and
Yousef were traveling together, but it could have
been known in short order, since Ajaj telephoned
constantly from prison and hectored Yousef about
the disposition of his luggage. All those calls were
duly recorded, but they were in Arabic, and, shockingly, weren't translated until much later. This is
another recurring theme in our domestic and international failures: Investigators and analysts repeatedly
lack the fundamental language and cultural skills necessary to assemble the basic facts. To get a sense of
the enormity of this failure, consider that it took nine
years for Ajaj's kit to be passed to the intelligence
community for analysis!

Our inability to understand what our enemies are
saying guarantees we will have a shortage of leads and
clues. Most people still do not realize that the World
Trade Center plot was hatched in the prison cell of
the man who murdered Rabbi Meir Kahane a few
months earlier. That man was known to go target
shooting—with AK-47s, no less—with two men who
later participated in the bombing operation. For ex-
tras, all were linked to the Abu Nidal global network.
Much of the plotting was done on the telephone, but
either no one was listening, or no one understood
what was being said. Afterward, the FBI discovered

that Yousef had spent many months in a safe house in Pakistan that was part of the bin Laden network. Finally, many of the Arabic-language documents used in the prosecution of the World Trade Center criminals were poorly translated, and the English versions diminished the central role of radical Islamic organizations. This aspect was not properly appreciated until outside scholars were brought in to check the translations and help with the analysis.

The lack of language skills goes hand in hand with another closely-realted cause of the domestic failure. One of the reasons the Bureau did not have enough translators on hand was that FBI manpower was geared to the kind of criminal activity they were used to fighting. If you wanted to go after the Mafia, you needed Italians and Italo-Americans who could credibly pose as *mafiosi*; if you were targeting black or Latino gangs, you needed African Americans who were comfortable with the street argot, or native Spanish speakers; if you were tracking down Soviet-bloc intelligence operations, you needed men and women fluent in Russian, Bulgarian, Romanian, and Polish. The FBI had all of these, and the government spent a small fortune on famous institutions like the Navy's Monterey Language School to ensure we had enough of them.

But we didn't have Arabs and Iranians.

This is a breathtaking failure. America is the

world's great melting pot. Whatever expertise you are looking for can be found in our population. When we went into Afghanistan in 2001, most Americans were astonished to discover that some of our uniformed military spoke Pashtu. They might be even more surprised to learn that approximately 53,000 Pashtu speakers live in the United States, and almost all of them are citizens. If we can deal with a relatively obscure tongue like Pashtu, it ought to be child's play to find Arabic and Farsi speakers, whether we want them to be translators or CIA case officers or FBI agents.

We chose not to, and the fundamental reason is politics. Both political parties contributed mightily to our failure, over many years. Every American president since Jimmy Carter has declared war on terrorism, but Carter, Reagan, the first Bush, and Clinton found it politically inopportune to aggressively wage that war. Indeed, most of our political leaders have devoted far more energy to *thwarting* an effective counterterrorist program within the United States than to insisting upon effective self-defense.

In the aftermath of September 11, critics lambasted the FBI and the CIA for their manifest incompetence and demanded quick action from them. But a problem created over several decades cannot be solved in a matter of a few months. The FBI and the CIA had acquired habits of mind and action that prevented American intelligence officers from pursuing potentially dangerous people and organizations. These self-defeating practices were not created by the intelligence agencies themselves. They were imposed on the American intelligence community by Congressional leaders, some of whom were among those who loudly demanded accountability and reform after September 11.

Listen to Oliver "Buck" Revell, who until he left Washington in 1991 was one of the FBI's best, rising to the rank of associate deputy director for investigations:

> In the late 1970s, the FBI practically shut down its entire domestic security operation. It was dealing with specific criminal acts after the fact and had virtually no collection, analysis, or utilization of intelligence prior to the commission of any sort of violent action by a politically motivated organization.[6]

The FBI was forced to dismantle its domestic security operations following highly publicized scandals investigated and broadcast by two Congressional committees: the (Senator Frank) Church Committee and the (Representative Otis) Pike Committee. The intelligence agencies were often portrayed as antidemocratic rogue organizations that desperately needed caging. In the wake of these Watergate-linked investigations, the Bureau and the CIA drastically reduced their investigations. Limits were defined by new guidelines as well as by presidential executive orders.

The guidelines and executive orders often prevented effective investigations of openly anti-American groups. The FBI, for example, was not even permitted to assemble files of newspaper clippings about groups loudly declaring their intention to wage violent war against the United States, nor could FBI agents simply listen to speeches at public meetings or rallies. Some members of Congress said that such actions reminded them of the behavior of political police. In order to conduct a serious investigation the FBI was required to prove the existence of a "criminal predicate." If they didn't have convincing evidence that a given group had either committed a crime or was plotting to commit one, they couldn't investigate.

This was a classic Catch-22 created by setting the "criminal" bar impossibly high. By setting such a high standard it's often impossible to have convincing proof of criminal intent or activity without investigating suspicious groups and individuals. While it is clearly necessary to limit the chances of abuse by governmental agencies, those agencies cannot defend the general welfare without pursuing legitimate leads. The question, then as now, is where to draw the line between serious investigation and political intimidation. In the immediate post-Watergate atmosphere, American politicians preferred to err on the side of limiting the activities of the FBI and the CIA.

Congress was warned at the time that hamstrung intelligence agencies would not be able to perform well, and this proved especially true in the field of counterterrorism. To go back to the World Trade Center bombing yet again, there was plenty of evidence showing that Meir Kahane's assassin was not a lone nut, but part of an international terror network. Had the leads been pursued, they might well have led investigators straight to the terror masters in the Middle East. The leads were not pursued, both because of the lack of the requisite language skills already discussed, and also because the post-Watergate rules had severely limited the ability of the FBI to dig deeply into matters involving free speech, politics, or religion.

I worked at the National Security Council in the mid-1980s, when the Red Brigades were terrorizing Italy. On a trip to Rome, I was told by Italian counterterrorist officials that one of the most infamous Italian terrorist leaders was headed for Cambridge, Massachusetts, where his girlfriend was attending Harvard summer school. Could the FBI keep an eye on this character? He might meet with some interesting people, and the Italian authorities would be most grateful for any such information.

Italy was a NATO ally, and terrorism was a major

threat there. But when I asked an FBI official about it, he exploded at me. "Are you nuts? Has this guy done anything criminal in the United States? Is there any reason to believe he's going to commit a crime here? No way!" There was no criminal predicate, so they could not watch the Italian terrorist.

The Italian request came at a difficult time for the Bureau, because they were in the grips of another scandal, this one related to an FBI investigation of a leftist group in the United States working to support radical change in El Salvador. It wasn't much, as scandals go. There had been no wiretaps, no bugs, no special surveillance. There were a couple of technical violations of the guidelines—some reports were filed late, for example—and an FBI agent had apparently pilfered money intended for an informant. The Bureau had recognized the improprieties and had shut down the investigation and opened an investigation of the agent. But once again FBI officials were testifying on live television, and Congressional investigators were alleging that the Bureau had slipped its leash.

The case against the FBI was largely smoke and mirrors, but the Reagan administration was not in a mood to fight yet another political battle when the Iran–Contra investigations were in high gear. Iran–Contra was aimed directly at the president. The Bureau would have to fend for itself. That was asking a lot of the new FBI chief, Judge William Sessions, who predictably but unfortunately took the position that since the alleged malfeasance had happened before he got there, he'd just apologize, promise to be more virtuous than Bill Webster had been, and ingratiate himself with Congress.

Like all organizations, the FBI and the CIA are molded by the character of their leaders, and if the maximum leader can't or won't stand up to political attack, the organization loses nerve and turns inward. Sessions's testimony severely damaged the morale of the FBI. Not only did he fail to defend the Bureau, he also confessed he wasn't even aware that the FBI was the lead organization in both counterintelligence and counterterrorism. Years later, when Sessions was forced to resign after allegations were made that he and his wife had improperly used FBI cars and employees for their private activities, a great sigh of satisfaction went through the upper ranks of the Bureau.

But the damage was done. Caught in the crossfire between political harassment and weak leadership, the FBI dropped anything that might be controversial, and concentrated narrowly on law enforcement. Revell remarks that in the late eighties "we almost went down to ground zero in carrying out our counterterrorism responsibilities," and believes that the combination of weak leadership from Sessions and the debilitating attacks from Congress contributed mightily to the terrible failure to detect the World Trade Center conspiracy.

It's hard to see the internal degeneration of a big organization like the FBI, even if you're inside it. That is why the American public was so surprised to discover that the FBI was not on top of the domestic terrorist threat. The main external clue was the Bureau's gradual transformation from an investigative agency acting to protect us against future attacks, into yet another law-enforcement group that investigated crimes once they had taken place. By 1993, even those FBI agents who believed that the Trade Center bombing was linked to Iraq had no inclination to pursue the leads. They focused their attention on getting indictments and then convictions.[7] The FBI was the key government agency in combating terrorism, but it had lost its mission.

If you wanted to know about the terror masters' American operations in those years, and for years to come, you would have been well advised—as the FBI's Buck Revell has unhesitatingly admitted—to ignore the Bureau's classified material and read the excellent work of Steven Emerson,[8] or Yehudit Barsky at the Anti-Defamation League,[9] or Yigal Carmon,[10] formerly counterterrorist adviser to Israel's prime minister. Top FBI officials willingly confirm that they enormously benefited from such researchers.

Neither the FBI nor local police seemed to know, for example, that both Hamas and Islamic Jihad— the fundamentalist organizations responsible for many of the suicide bomb attacks against Israel—had long operated in the United States. Both of them had placed major leaders within the American intellectual community without a ripple of protest. Ramadan Abdal Shallah had been on the academic staff of the University of South Florida before becoming the leader of Islamic Jihad, and Musa Abu Marzuq headed up the United Association for Studies and Research just outside Washington, D.C. before being arrested as one of Hamas's top killers in Israel. They worked closely with one another, with Marzuq the senior figure.

Theirs were major operations; Hamas and Jihad raised millions of dollars, distributed countless pieces of propaganda, and recruited warriors to the cause. The American offices also served as safe havens and operations centers. Arabic-language publications were edited in the U.S. and then faxed or e-mailed back to the Middle East. Even assassinations of suspected traitors within Hamas and Jihad were sometimes cleared with their American leaders before being carried out.

Even if we were to expel all the leaders today, there would still be a formidable presence in the United States. I recently asked a former top FBI

official how many Americans he thought had participated in the Islamic campaigns of the past decade or
so, including Bosnia, Kosovo, and Afghanistan. He
said, "Thousands." Most of them came home afterward, waiting to fight again another day, as John Wal-
ker Lindh would probably have done (and as an
unknown number of his comrades-in-arms have undoubtedly done) if he had not been captured by
American Special Forces.

The demoralization of an intelligence service car-
ries a big price tag, even if the bill doesn't come due
for several years. By the time this bill came due in
America in the mid-nineties, the country needed a
first-class FBI, but it had lost its bearings. As a result,
we missed what is probably the biggest story of all:
the creation of a fundamentalist Islamic network
within the United States under cover of a religious
movement.

Those thousands of American Muslims who went
to wage their jihad overseas had studied in radical
Islamic schools, and prayed in radical Islamic
mosques in the United States. They were filled with
hate for all infidels, told of the glories awaiting warriors in the holy war, then sent overseas for training.
Indoctrination and information came through radical
mosques and radical schools, rarely if ever investigated, except by enterprising journalists and scholars.
Those who looked into the curricula of our Islamic

schools found that all students were required to read hate-filled literature as a matter of routine. For example, an eleventh-grade textbook used in the Islamic Saudi Academy in suburban Washington, D.C., taught that "One sign of the Day of Judgment will be that Muslims will fight and kill Jews, who will hide behind trees that say, 'Oh Muslim, Oh servant of God, here is a Jew hiding behind me. Come here and kill him.' "

Those who have investigated have found much to worry about. The mosques and schools serve as distribution points for fundamentalist hate literature, and bring into American education the same vicious anti-Semitic and anti-American texts that are used throughout the Middle East. Most of the textbooks are Wahhabi, paid for by the Saudis, but others come from different terror masters. An Iranian-American imam named Muhammad al-Asi was for several years the head of the Muslim Community School and the Islamic Education Center in Potomac, Maryland, a posh community north of Washington, D.C. He was also briefly the imam at the Islamic Center in Washington itself and, according to Steven Emerson, "he still preaches on the sidewalk outside on Fridays."[11] The Islamic Education Center distributes literature direct from Tehran, including the Ayatollah Khomeini's celebrated death sentence on the novelist Salman Rushdie. It also sells anti-Semitic tapes from

Switzerland that praise Khomeini as a latter-day Hitler. Al-Asi has been honored at an official dinner in Tehran, with Iran's supreme leader, the Ayatollah Khamene'i presiding.

These radical Islamic schools and mosques in the United States are not products of American religious thought or even, for the most part, of Americans' money. Most of the mosques and schools are inspired by the radical Saudi version of Islam known as Wahhabism, on which more later. And most of the money also comes from Saudi Arabia. The American Sufi leader Sheik Hisham Kabbani, who founded the Islamic Supreme Council of America to combat the influence of the Wahhabis in the United States, testified at a State Department hearing that 80 percent of the nation's mosques were under Wahhabi influence or outright control. The numbers bear him out. A majority of the roughly 1,200 mosques in the United States were built in the last fifteen years, and a large part of the money came from Saudi Arabia to spread the Wahhabi faith. Those who have studied this phenomenon most closely estimate that the Saudis have spent several billion dollars on the worldwide network of mosques and schools.

These are breeding grounds for future terrorists, but they are even more dangerous than that. In some cases they are actual pieces of the terror network itself. FBI officers of my acquaintance are certain that some of the Wahhabi mosques in the United States have been vital links in the logistical and communications chain that enabled the overseas terror masters to control, instruct and perhaps even pay their agents in this country.

This network explains what to me was the most astonishing fact about September 11: the control mechanism exercised over the terrorists. Many of the terrorists had lived among us for considerable time; in some cases for several years. The United States is a famously corrupting country. We take all manner of foreigners and turn them into Americans in remarkably short order; not for nothing are we known as a cultural and ethnic melting pot. Yet these people lived among us, worked with us, went to restaurants, bars, and nightclubs with us, and remained full of hate for us. How did they manage to maintain their separateness? How could the terror masters back in Tehran, Baghdad, Damascus, and the caves of Afghanistan be confident that their orders would be carried out?

In the cases of Palestinian suicide terrorism in Israel, the uncertainty of control is palpable. The handlers stay with the young martyr-to-be until the very last minute, and even so there are many defections once the terrorists arrive at their scheduled death point. Moreover, the Palestinian suicide bombers are young, and therefore more easily manipulated than older people—like Mohammed Atta and the others of September 11, who were mature men from wealthy and esteemed families and who were well educated and could have had successful careers either in their own countries or overseas. Even though they had been thoroughly indoctrinated, there had to be some means of psychological reinforcement—of projecting discipline—to provide sufficient control to headquarters.

The mosques served that function. The sheikhs and imams in the hundreds of Wahhabi and Shi'ite mosques in America reinforced the incantation of jihad, and supported a community of fundamentalist believers in which the terrorists could immerse themselves. The constant emphasis on jihad maintained the state of passionate commitment with which the terrorists arrived in America, and a friend of mine who knows the terror network firsthand insists that "you cannot think about these people the way you think about yourself and your friends. They really wanted to die. They hated living in America, and the phone call was a release for them; they didn't have to contaminate themselves anymore. They could kill thousands of infidels and go to paradise."

The terror masters overseas were confident in the reliability of the killers in America because they had never let their terrorist agents escape psychological control. The key mechanism was the control of the terrorists' minds, and it was maintained by the mosques. The mosques—firmly in the hands of like-minded fanatics—constantly reinforced the hatred in their sermons and through abundant printed materials. In the first days after September 11, I wondered if we had finally seen an example of the "Manchurian candidate," killers so totally brainwashed and programmed that when the phone call came, they simply moved like robots to carry out their assignments.

To be sure, there are important differences between the hypnotized killers of *The Manchurian Candidate* and the Muslim fanatics of September 11. The 9/11 terrorists weren't hypnotically transformed from normal people to disciplined killers. Some were indoctrinated from their earliest years, much like the young Nazis who accepted suicidal missions for the Fuhrer in the second World War. Others converted to fundamentalist Islam later in life. But the manipulation of the human soul that was so chillingly portrayed in the early Cold War movie was raised to the level of an art form by the terror masters.

Those American officials now charged with protecting us against future terrorist attacks worry a lot about the ability of this network of schools and mosques to create substantial numbers of deranged American followers. In his elegant, understated way, V. S. Naipaul well understands the psychological pro-

cess that takes place in the minds of the young believers:

> Islam is not simply a matter of conscience
> or private belief. It makes imperial demands.
> A convert's worldview alters. His holy
> places are in Arab lands; his sacred language
> is Arabic. His idea of history alters. He re-
> jects his own; he becomes, whether he likes
> it or not, a part of the Arab story. The con-
> vert has to turn away from everything that
> is his. The disturbance for societies is im-
> mense, and even after a thousand years can
> remain unresolved; the turning away has to
> be done again and again. People develop
> fantasies about who and what they are; and
> in the Islam of converted countries there is
> an element of neurosis and nihilism. These
> countries can be easily set on the boil.[12]

This is another tough problem for American leaders.
They know the network of schools and mosques is
dangerous to our national security, since it both cre-
ates and supports radical Islamic fundamentalists and
even terrorists.

Yet we are committed to the protection of free
speech, no matter how odious it may be, and to the
protection of religion, however foreign it may seem.

Just as the FBI must constantly find an acceptable boundary between the government's need to investigate and the individual's right to live undisturbed, so top officials at the Department of Justice are looking for a way to limit the effect of radical Islamic doctrines without violating the sanctity of free speech and religion.

One of our greatest jurists, Justice Oliver Wendell Holmes, decades ago asserted that the state can limit certain kinds of speech under extreme circumstances: "a man can not shout 'fire' in a crowded theater."

In all likelihood, the Justice Department will opt to finesse the problem and use the "Al Capone solution." Unable to convict the Mafia boss for his most serious crimes, the government sent him to prison for income tax violations. Perhaps the Bush Administration will find a way to prosecute the American Islamic fundamentalists for some activity that involves neither speech nor religion.

Clinton

To repeat, every president since Jimmy Carter has declared war on terrorism, but none of them waged it seriously before September 11, 2001. That suggests that our failure to adequately prepare for the terrorists' assault is not simply due to bad leadership. There is something about America itself that makes us vulnerable to foreign attack.

America has rarely been prepared for war, above all because of our lucky geography. Not only do we have two sizeable oceans separating us from potential European and Asian enemies, but we have Canadians and Mexicans across our borders. American leaders could afford a calculated insouciance toward national security. If war broke out overseas, our leaders could take their time deciding whether to intervene. Even after Pearl Harbor, there was no further Japanese or German assault against American territory, and the Roosevelt administration was left undisturbed for many months to build American military power, train American soldiers, and design American strategies.

Moreover, unsophisticated in the ways of other peoples and nations, Americans have long believed in the basic goodness of mankind, and therefore that war was something unnatural and temporary. Our radical egalitarianism, enshrined in our most cherished documents, leads us to treat all people the same way, and to grant foreign cultures the same respect and standing as our own. Thus, even when America's enemies openly tell us how much they hate us, and what great pleasure they will take from killing us, our first instinct is to wonder what we have done to offend them, and how we might convince them of our basic goodness. Back when the Ayatollah Khomeini was inciting the Shi'ite masses of Iran to overthrow the shah, the Reverend Andrew Young, then our ambassador to the United Nations, remarked that Khomeini couldn't be all bad, since he was "a religious man."

Having misunderstood so much about human nature and the true nature of human history, America and its leaders typically ignore unpleasant evidence. It was easy to get inside Adolf Hitler's mind; all you had to do was read *Mein Kampf*. Likewise, Khomeini's and bin Laden's sermons and commentaries and other incitements were either in print or recorded on audio cassettes. Both eventually delivered their unpleasant surprises in a form we could no longer ignore. Yet our leaders resist the obvious conclusions: that the world is full of frustrated, fanatical, and nasty people, that we are hated by many groups in many countries around the world, and that they're going to come after us. So we'd better be ready, or, best of all, get them first. Instead, our leaders have demobilized after the end of every war, and are never ready for the next war, whether it be a ground war in Europe or a terrorist war at home and abroad.

Which is to say that many of President Clinton's failures were quintessentially American. What set him apart was his inability to recognize a real war even when faced with one, even when Americans were being killed. His immediate predecessors—Carter,

Reagan, and Bush the Father—had to cope with terrorist attacks against American targets overseas, and
so long as it was something distant, their unwillingness to mount an effective response was understandable, albeit unfortunate. Moreover, Carter and
Reagan had the Soviet Union to contend with, and
Bush the Father was engaged in actual warfare in Kuwait, Somalia, and Panama.

Clinton's circumstances were quite different. After initial skirmishes in Haiti and Somalia (the latter,
in retrospect, a significant event in the terror war,
because Osama bin Laden trained some of the fighters who killed American soldiers in Mogadishu),
there were no major foreign policy crises to deflect
his attention from terrorism. And, beginning a month
after his inauguration (the Trade Center was bombed
in February 1993), Clinton was formally accountable
for our lack of response to terrorist assaults on American soil.

There were plenty of those, from the World Trade
Center to the plot, discovered shortly thereafter, to
bomb the United Nations and the Lincoln and Holland Tunnels, from Oklahoma City to the explosives
en route from Canada to to Los Angeles for a millennium big bang, from the 1998 simultaneous
bombing of our embassies in Kenya and Tanzania (an
attack against sovereign American territory) to the
suicide bombing of the USS *Cole* in the port of Aden
the following year.

This dramatic escalation of the terror war was staged on Clinton's watch. He was responsible for fighting and defeating it, which he failed to do. Indeed, he did the opposite. Clinton actively pardoned terrorists—the Puerto Rican bombers shortly before the Senatorial election in New York (with its sizeable Latino voting bloc), and two more, female radical leftists from the seventies, in his disgraceful final hours in the White House. Unwilling to deal effectively with the issue, Clinton appointed blue ribbon commissions to stall for time, hoping things would improve by themselves. Reagan had appointed one himself, chaired by Vice President Bush, and Clinton followed suit, naming Al Gore to head a group to study problems in airline and airport security. There were two further commissions on terrorism, the latest—which reported in 2000—under former State Department terrorist coordinator Paul Bremer. While there were some variations, all four commissions sang from the same hymnal: Terrorism was serious and must be dealt with seriously.

Everyone who looked at terrorism soon realized that it was only a matter of time before the terrorists got their hands on weapons of mass destruction and it was folly to wait for that to happen. Recommendations varied, but most agreed that we had to tighten our border controls, remove some of the restrictions on our intelligence services, go proactive against the terrorists and the states that harbored, aided, or sponsored them, improve information sharing among the myriad federal, state, and local agencies entrusted with our security, and drastically improve security at airports and around our critical sites—from power plants and bridges to telecommunications networks and private computer nets, etc.

Clinton was unmoved. A few minor improvements were adopted, but nothing serious was done. The president never even visited the '93 World Trade Center bombing site.

Meanwhile, despite all our intelligence agencies' built-in shortcomings, government counterterrorist officials were slowly assembling a clearer picture of the enemy forces. Bit by bit, they became aware that we were indeed under attack. By the beginning of Clinton's second term in 1996, top government officials were openly warning of a big terrorist attack within the United States. John O'Neill, the FBI's colorful and able counterterrorist chief, said so in a speech in 1997, and his prediction was borne out in the circumstances of his own demise. O'Neill went to work as security chief for the World Trade Center in the fall of 2001, where he was killed by the terrorists on September 11.

In fact, we were not totally at the mercy of the terrorists; we had our victories along the way. Clinton ordered a vast operation for the millennium celebration, and it headed off planned Al Qaeda attacks both here and in Jordan. There were even some moves against bin Laden himself, leading to his relocation from Sudan to Afghanistan, a move that strengthened him, even though at the time—1996—the administration viewed it as a success for our side.

But Clinton was not driven to take the kind of action the situation demanded. Not that he had all the tools for the job; as will be shown, the CIA was no better than the Bureau. Crucial information was lacking, and both the CIA and the FBI had pulled in their investigative horns and were minding all the p's and q's of their restrictive guidelines. And, in keeping with the established pattern of excessive and moralistic legalism overcoming common sense, foolishly high standards of evidence were repeatedly used by both political and legal advisers to frustrate sensible action. National leaders must often make difficult decisions based on evidence that might not convince a judge and jury beyond a reasonable doubt. But Clinton's advisers insisted that it would be wrong, for example, to arrest terrorist leaders, even ringleaders like Osama bin Laden, unless we were certain to win a conviction from a jury in the District of Columbia.

So Clinton had abundant excuses to take very limited and largely symbolic steps against the terrorists, even though the evidence of danger was substantial, and even though his political guru, Dick Morris, warned him that he was very vulnerable to Republican accusations of being soft on terrorism. Morris believed that a big slice of the electorate—maybe as much as 7 percent—would rally to Clinton if he ordered tough action.

As always with Clinton, the overriding reasons for action or inaction were personal. The political considerations were inconclusive, because there were arguments for and against strong action. He might win seven points in the next election if he smashed Al Qaeda and ordered enhanced security within the United States, but he didn't really think he needed those points—Bob Dole and Jack Kemp certainly did not seem to be a serious threat to his reelection in '96. On the other hand, a serious effort to combat the terror masters might have automatically provoked cries of protest from major elements of Clinton's coalition. Shut down the bank accounts of terrorist front organizations? Bad, because, as Treasury Secretary Rubin argued, it would send shock waves through the world's financial organizations, and we were the guarantors of international financial stability. Link the expiration of visas to the duration of drivers' licenses—a measure that might have caught Mohammed Atta? No, George Stephanopoulos argued, because it would annoy the Democrats' Latino base. Give airline security people access to a "watch list" of suspected terrorists, so they might be caught if they traveled under their own names? Good idea, but a nuisance. It was never implemented.

Then there was the "legacy" matter, and the much desired Nobel prize for bringing peace to the Middle East. No matter how you approached it, a fight against the terror masters inevitably meant a fight against the enemies of Israel, and no doubt the foreign policy team feared that the president would thus appear to have tilted toward the Jewish state at a time when he was desperately trying to be even-handed. Even a limited response, aimed solely against foreign terrorists on American soil, would automatically put the administration at odds with the terrorists' home bases in the Middle East. It was all too easy for Clinton, Berger, Cohen, and Albright to convince themselves that terrorism would be easier to deal with, once they had accomplished a durable peace between Israel and the PLO.

The Clinton administration thereby inverted the real problem, for it was and is impossible to achieve a Middle Eastern peace by focusing solely on the Palestinian-Israeli conflict. The terrorist assault against Israel was not merely a Palestinian strategy. It was fully supported by the terror masters in Syria, Iran, and Iraq, and generously funded by Saudi Arabia. And it was not merely an attack against Israel; the terror masters have long aimed to eliminate the American presence in the region. Thus peace could not be achieved without dealing with Iran, Iraq, Syria, and Saudi Arabia. But Clinton did not want to go to war against the terror masters. He strained to avoid conflict with the terror states at all costs. The international aspects of Clinton's behavior will be treated at greater length in the next chapter, but one domestic action bears mention here:

> The Clinton administration shut down a 1995 investigation of Islamic charities, concerned that a public probe would expose Saudi Arabia's suspected ties to a global money-laundering operation that raised millions for anti-Israel terrorists . . .
>
> Law enforcement authorities and others close to the aborted investigation said the State Department pressed federal officials to pull agents off the previously undisclosed probe after the charities were targeted in the diversion of cash to groups that fund terrorism.[13]

The investigation had turned up more than a billion dollars in Saudi contributions to four interlinked Islamic "foundations, institutes, and charities" in northern Virginia. A former federal prosecutor said that if the operation had been shut down, "they would have been unable to raise the millions that since have been used by terrorists in hundreds of suicide attacks." In late March 2002, the Bush administration shut down many of the same organizations that had been targeted in 1995.

In cases like this one, it is very difficult to argue that Clinton lacked sufficient information to act against the terror masters. The American government had abundant information, and would have acquired much more if federal prosecutors had been permitted to shut down the Islamic organizations. Clinton prevented the Justice Department from acting on the information it had, and blocked its efforts to strike a meaningful blow against the terror network.

The best explanation for Clinton's behavior was given five hundred years ago by Niccolò Machiavelli, who had great contempt for leaders lacking military virtue. He knew that weak leaders, especially those who became personally corrupt and thus inordinately self-indulgent, were never willing to fight seriously. Such leaders, he said, shrink from real combat, and the only time they use military force is to look good. They will never order a real assault against their enemies, because they are unwilling to accept the risk of defeat. Men of this sort, like Clinton, prefer to play it safe, and either take half measures or simply pretend to act.

He calls such weak-kneed men "indolent princes," and, in *The Art of War*, Machiavelli describes a generation of indolent Italian leaders just before they were crushed by ambitious foreign invaders. His description reads as if it had been crafted to describe the Clinton Administration.

> They thought . . . that it sufficed for a prince in the writing-rooms of palaces to think up a sharp reply, to write a beautiful letter, to demonstrate wit and readiness in saying and words, to know how to weave a fraud . . . to keep many lascivious women around, to conduct himself avariciously and proudly, to rot in idleness, to give military rank by favor, to be scornful if anyone might show them any praiseworthy path, to want their words to be oracular responses, nor did these no-accounts realize that they were preparing themselves to be the prey of whoever assaulted them . . . [14]

It was simply not in the president's character to wage effective war against the terror masters, especially when he had the perfect weapon for the sort of thing he had in mind: the cruise missile. Launched from a safe distance (so no American lives were at risk) and spectacular to watch (thereby enhancing his own glory), cruise missiles produced the illusion of war without risking the real thing.

Whenever possible, Clinton simply ignored annoying national security questions like terrorism. Just ask poor Jim Woolsey, Clinton's first director of Central Intelligence, who quit in disgust after failing for two full years to engage the president on national security matters.[15]

Clinton might have been saved from his own worst instincts, if he'd had national security advisers who forced him to deal seriously with terrorism. But none of them was so inclined.

That left Woolsey's successors at the CIA as the last best hope. Their strengths and shortcomings will occupy our attention in much of the next chapter; for now, suffice it to say that it was a feeble hope indeed. John Deutch, a distinguished scientist and former deputy secretary of defense, was certainly not going to insist on action because he didn't think there was much of a threat, and he wanted to reshape the CIA to deal with more "modern" problems. He was followed by George Tenet, a skilled Washington hand who had gone to the Agency as Deutch's deputy after years on the staff of the Senate's Select Committee on Intelligence, and who remains atop the Agency. Unlike Woolsey, Tenet had a good rapport with Clinton (and has an even better relationship with President Bush). Unlike Deutch, he did not wish to reinvent the intelligence community. Although a lifelong Democrat, he came from the center of the party, and no one doubted his intense patriotism.

By the time Tenet moved up to the top job, it

should have been clear that the United States was in the crosshairs of the terror masters. The CIA is supposed to know all about such people, and to get inside the terror network so that our national leaders know what the terrorists are planning to do to us.

It didn't happen, and George Tenet must shoulder his share of the blame for September 11. But it certainly wasn't all due to Tenet or his immediate predecessors. As with the FBI, it took time to weaken our foreign intelligence service. And as with the Bureau, there's blame aplenty, from Congress to the press, from weak directors to analysts wearing blinders.

3

THE FOREIGN THEATER

(The CIA) probably doesn't have a single truly qualified Arabic-speaking officer of Middle Eastern background who can play a believable Muslim fundamentalist.

—REUEL GERECHT, QUOTING A FORMER CIA OFFICIAL

Back in the mid-eighties, as the Cold War was nearing its end, the great Soviet dissident Vladimir Bukovsky went out to CIA headquarters to propose a scheme to the Agency's director, William Casey. Bukovsky laid it out, and Casey was enthusiastic. "Terrific," he said, "one of the best I've ever heard. It ought to work, it should be done." Bukovsky was understandably delighted, and awaited his instructions. But instead Casey leaned forward and, almost whispering, said, "Let me give you some advice. Don't tell the CIA about it; they'll fuck it up."

Casey was the last great director of Central Intelligence, a legend in his own time because he had all the qualities required for the post. He had operational experience (having served in OSS during the second World War), he knew politics and business (having run Reagan's presidential election campaign, and having been the head of the Securities and Exchange Commission), and he had the ear of the president. Moreover, he had the street smarts of a lifelong New Yorker, and a restless curiosity that challenged the finest intellects. When he traveled, which was often, he ransacked bookstores all over the world, constantly looking for new sources of information and new ways to understand what was going on. The CIA is notoriously insular, but Casey was the opposite. He always had time for outsiders who could stimulate him and get him to think outside the Agency's top-secret envelope.

Everybody knew that the CIA was in a bad way; that's why Reagan sent Casey there. The CIA had undergone the same battering as the FBI, except more so. Both had been excoriated by Congress in the Pike and Church Commission hearings, and the CIA underwent a considerable internal purge during the latter years of Richard Nixon's unhappy presidency. Then Jimmy Carter had appointed Admiral

Stansfield Turner as DCI, which was a further blow. In keeping with the populist tone of the new administration, Turner vowed to make the CIA "more like America," by which he meant that Agency personnel should become more diverse, with women and minorities given more opportunities. This led to some hilarious results, as when a would-be agent in Communist central Europe went to meet a CIA case officer in an outdoor café, only to discover that the Agency had sent a very tall, very black man who attracted considerable attention. The agent-to-be promptly hightailed it out of there.

Turner continued the purge, shutting down eight hundred positions in the clandestine service, and driving more than three hundred others into early retirement. And he chose the worst possible method for an organization whose performance depends greatly on morale. Instead of asking senior officers to make the painful choices themselves, and working with the victims to ease their transition (for no other reason than the concern that some of them might be angry enough to offer their services to the enemy), Turner had the list randomly generated by computer.

Resentment in the ranks was so great that Turner was nicknamed "Captain Queeg" by his colleagues, and in January 1979, some wit at the Agency distributed a bogus issue of the Director's "Notes" to all employees. The hoax recounted how Turner/Queeg had discovered that somebody had stolen his favorite strawberries, and continued:

> I am therefore ordering that until the strawberries are returned to my refrigerator, no one will leave the building. The General Services Administration will be asked to augment meal service while we wait. As an added stimulus I am riffing 100 people per day until the wrong is righted. Any person helping to identify the thief will, beside an immediate quality step increase, be given a pair of stainless steel spheres similar to those I use for thinking the unpalatable thoughts our Communist adversaries force us to think. . . . [1]

This was the dysfunctional organization Bill Casey took over in early 1981.

Things were particularly difficult in counterterrorism. As with the FBI, the scandals of the mid-seventies had led to strict guidelines for the behavior of CIA case officers, and Turner's purge of the clandestine service was driven by these new rules, combined with wide-ranging scrutiny from numerous Congressional oversight committees (at one point more than two hundred members of Congress had access to the CIA's most highly classified information) and the press. The most daunting new rule came in the form of Executive Order #11905, signed by President Gerald Ford on February 18, 1976, and renewed by every successive administration. This act forbade the government from engaging in assassinations, and over time government lawyers spun out a series of implications: We could not assassinate, or cause to assassinate, or get involved with assassins. All of which made it very difficult to recruit agents inside terrorist organizations, because murder was their business.

The legalistic interpretation of the executive order was so daunting that CIA case officers were forced to abandon agents if it became likely the agent would participate in lethal action. This produced the worst possible outcome. Young radicals who might be inclined to cooperate with the United States would only run the risk if they were confident we would protect them if things got dicey. The new regs guaranteed that they would be abandoned at the most sensitive moment, which in turn guaranteed that we wouldn't get any more recruits.

We tied ourselves in an elegant and very tight knot: The FBI couldn't keep files of newspaper stories, and the CIA couldn't talk to terrorists. No wonder our intelligence was so bad.

But Casey was a different story. Recognizing that we simply had to find a legal way to penetrate the terror network, the CIA found ways to get it done. To be sure, some of the operations were so complicated that they defy the imagination—as when agents had to stage simulated attacks and bombings, all the while guaranteeing that nobody got hurt— but the CIA began to get some decent agents in the eighties.

> ... innovative means of maintaining a recruit within a terrorist organization—short of shooting somebody—were permissible. On a number of occasions, we staged operations that pretty much followed the . . . instructions to our agent, but were totally scripted and controlled by us. No one got hurt . . . [2]

In addition to finding imaginative ways to recruit terrorists, Casey effectively addressed another big problem: The very structure of the intelligence community made it hard to develop a clear picture of the terror masters. From its creation, the CIA had been "compartmentalized." Each intelligence compartment did its own specialized work—the analysts analyzed, the case officers recruited, the National Security Agency intercepted communications, the satellites transmitted their images—but the entire package could never arrive in one place so that professional analysts could see the whole picture. Furthermore, the Agency, like the State Department, was organized geographically, and terrorism wasn't.

> [Terrorism] is effective precisely because it spreads all over the map. An Arab terrorist group may be based in Libya or Syria, but its operations are likely to take place in Rome or London or Athens. . . . Which division has jurisdiction—the Near East or Europe? Geographic divisions of responsibility create jurisdictional and coordination squabbles that play right into terrorists' hands.[3]

When the American embassy and then the Marine barracks in Beirut were blown up in 1983, with hundreds killed, including several top CIA people, Casey was furious. One of the Agency's best, Bob Ames, had been visiting Beirut and was killed in the blast, his death verified by the discovery of a left hand with his wedding ring on the fourth finger. Casey called for a detailed, all-sources damage assessment, in which, for the first time, all the information was analyzed. It turned out that there was plenty of good intelligence on the terrorists who did the terrible deeds (for example, we "knew" that the terrorists had built a model of the Marine barracks in a Lebanese valley, and practiced blowing it up). If we had looked at, listened to, and analyzed it all, we certainly could have seen it coming. Our own organizational chart had done us in.

So Casey instructed Dewey Clarridge, one of the best case officers in the Agency, a hard-driving, independent-minded man with extensive experience in the Middle East and a first-class bureaucrat to boot, to create a counterterrorist center where all the intelligence on terrorism came together.

It worked, and fairly quickly produced a spectacular success. Clarridge and his associates were able to assemble an amazingly complete picture of the Abu Nidal gang, and then waged psychological warfare against him. They repeatedly approached his agents and offered to pay them to work for the United States. The Agency publicly exposed the names of his commercial intermediaries and bankers. All this took a terrible toll:

> . . . Those who reported having been approached by us were not rewarded for their loyalty, because Abu Nidal never quite believed that anyone in his group had turned us down. Their loyalty was suspect thereafter, and the punishment for disloyalty was torture and death.
>
> By 1987, a fearful Abu Nidal had turned

his terror campaign inward. . . . Accused followers were tortured to confess, then executed on the basis of that confession. . . .
Over three hundred hard-core operatives
were murdered (in Lebanon) on Abu Nidal's order. On a single night in November
1987, approximately 170 were tied up and
blindfolded, machine-gunned, and pushed
into a trench prepared for the occasion. Another 160 or so were killed in Libya shortly
thereafter . . . Abu Nidal's paranoia, fed by
our crusade against him, caused him to destroy his organization.[4]

Those gunned down got merciful deaths compared to those who were subjected to the ghastly tor-
tures of Abu Nidal. Victims were routinely buried
alive, fed through a tube lodged in their mouths, and
finally executed by a single bullet fired through the
feeding tube. Still others had their sexual organs
placed in skillets full of boiling oil.

The Counterterrorism Center was the most effective American effort against international terrorism in a generation,[5] a tribute to what can be done
when a good director of Central Intelligence finds a
top-notch and imaginative chief of counterterrorism, and gives him all the support he needs. Even
so, it was hardly a full-fledged war. Clarridge and

company shone in comparison with the bureaucratic gray of the Near East Division, but it was not the stuff of lore and legend. The really big time terrorist operations, like Hizbollah and the PLO, were hardly damaged.

The Counterterrorism Center's brief moment of limited success ended with the death of Casey and the purge of Clarridge in the Iran-Contra affair. Washington scandals produced many victims, regardless of culpability, and Clarridge was viewed as "Casey's guy." Since Casey was beyond the reach of earthly punishment, the inquisitors had to content themselves with Clarridge. Had they been at all interested in counterterrorism, the investigators would have found a much bigger scandal: our ignorance of the basic elements of Middle East terrorism.

Prior to our contacts with Iran in 1985, the intelligence community had only a very limited understanding of the extent to which Tehran was the driving force behind the murderous activities of Hizbollah. (For that matter, the CIA was shockingly ignorant about Iran in general. The "Iran desk officer" in the Operations Directorate—who spoke not a word of Farsi but nonetheless went on to great rewards culminating in London, the choicest CIA station in the world—had spent the bulk of his career in Latin America, and did not even know the names of the top government officials in Tehran.) Both

Casey and Reagan were determined to liberate the several American hostages in Lebanon, especially the Agency's own William Buckley, and the experts were divided between those who believed Hizbollah was an independent local organization, and those who thought it was strongly backed by the Syrian government.

While working as a consultant to the National Security Council in 1985, I was the first American official to meet with Iranian intermediaries, and some of them told me in the strongest language that Hizbollah was an Iranian creation, and that the only way one could arrange the release of hostages was by dealing with the Islamic Republic. The American experts doubted it, as did I, but the Iranians were right. There was simply no other way to explain the cause-and-effect relationship between arms sales to Iran and hostage releases by Hizbollah in Lebanon.

Our ignorance was only part of the problem; the CIA and other government officials showed a cavalier indifference to the fate of foreigners who helped us understand terrorism. In the course of our contacts with Iranians, we found a high-ranking terrorist leader who was willing to talk to the CIA and explain the workings of the Iranian terror network. CIA analysts told me that his information was extremely good, but in keeping with the eternal dictum that no good deed will go unpunished the poor man was sacrificed by the Tower Commission, headed by former Senators John Tower and Edmund Muskie and General Brent Scowcroft, the former (and later once again) national security adviser. For some reason, they felt obliged to put a reference to this person into their report, and, incredibly, included the man's name. No one with a proper sense of the importance of security could have permitted this to occur, yet no one at the CIA and no one on the Tower Commission insisted that the name remain secret. Predictably he was murdered shortly after publication of the report.

Lethal blunders of this sort produced immediate effects on the ground. It is very difficult to induce members of terrorist organizations to risk their lives by telling their secrets to the CIA if they know they may be exposed in a public document.

During our contacts with the Iranians, we got a pretty clear picture of Iran's leading role in international terrorism. But American policy makers did not want to hear it, because it implied a course of action that they were unwilling to adopt. If we concluded that Iran was behind the murders of hundreds of Americans, we would be obliged to act. Since we weren't prepared to work for the removal of the Khomeini regime, we ran from the evidence.

And there was another reason, which went to the heart of our Middle East diplomacy.

The PLO: Redefining Terrorism

For years, the Agency's primary interest in international terrorism was the Palestine Liberation Organization.[6] Yet in a closed hearing to Congressional oversight committees in the autumn of 1979, Agency experts argued that it was improper to term the PLO a "terrorist" organization, that the group was actually "moderate" and simply maintained a facade of terrorism to curry favor with "radical Arabs."

This benevolent view of the PLO was no doubt welcome to the diplomatic corps, then as now intent on advancing the "peace process" in the Middle East, and thus eager to accredit the PLO as a legitimate partner in that process—a major recurring theme. It was also a clever way to beat the restrictions flowing from the executive order: If you didn't think you were dealing with terrorists, it was okay to recruit PLO members. But the CIA assessment was dangerously misleading, for the PLO was a truly radical terrorist organization, and by far the most important—at least until the Israeli invasion of Lebanon in 1981. Moreover, it had played a secret role in assisting the Ayatollah Khomeini's seizure of power in Iran, and it worked intimately with the Iranian regime thereafter. This was a major development for two reasons: The Iranian revolution was the fundamental turning point in the history of international terror, and the Iran–PLO terrorist joint venture killed hundreds of Americans, including the Beirut embassy massacre of 1983.

Indeed, until the fall of the Soviet Empire—which removed the PLO's main sponsor—the PLO was the nerve center for international terrorism, Islamic and otherwise (radical Marxist groups have always played a significant role in Arafat's organization). Arafat worked hand in glove with Islamic radicals like the Muslim Brotherhood (of which both he and his father before him had been members), with Arab nationalists in Egypt and Syria, and with left-wing groups like Baader-Meinhof in Germany and the Red Brigades in Italy.

There was a terror network long before Osama bin Laden, and it worked much the way Al Qaeda would later. State sponsors provided the necessary territory, intelligence, and logistics, and groups with wildly differing world views helped one another against a common enemy. But every organization, even the most informal, requires leadership, and the PLO provided it. Without the PLO, terrorism would have been more easily manageable. With the PLO, terrorism became a major problem, particularly once the shah of Iran was overthrown and the Ayatollah Khomeini had taken over.

In 1972, seven years before the fall of the shah, PLO chief Yasser Arafat signed an agreement with

Khomeini to train the men who later became the hardcore of the Iranian Revolutionary Guards. From then on, the PLO and the Iranians were joined at the hip so far as terrorist operations were concerned, even though both took care to conceal their alliance. Both excelled at deception, and Arafat later bragged about his creation of the Abu Nidal group—which then carried out his instructions, even assassinating dissident PLO members—so that he could point to them and say, "Those are the radicals; I am a good moderate." This deception was modeled on a similar ruse pulled off by Romania's Communist dictator Nicolae Ceausescu, who successfully duped successive American presidents into believing that he, too, was a "moderate," in contrast to others that he in fact controlled.

The PLO deception has been remarkably successful for more than thirty years, even though there has long been abundant evidence that the PLO was at the very center of international terror, and that Iran and the PLO worked hand in glove. But the CIA's Middle East experts always found ways around admitting this dirty little secret. The CIA convinced itself that terrorism, like politics in general, was always local, and that terrorist groups were the expression of desperate rage against real or imagined injustices.

I first ran into this mind set when I moved from

Rome to Washington in 1977. I had been writing for *The New Republic* for several years, and the Red Brigades terrorists figured prominently in my stories. Most every informed person in Italy "knew"—simply because it was so obvious—that the Red Brigades had come out of the dark underbelly of the Italian Communist Party, and that they therefore had some kind of working relationship with the Soviet intelligence services. One of the founders of the Red Brigades, the Communist publisher Giangiacomo Feltrinelli, had gone back and forth to Prague a dozen times in a very few years, and Prague was famous as the place where clandestine members of the Italian Communist Party went for rest, instructions, training and money. The Brigades' "revolutionary" language reeked of old-fashioned Leninism, and one of the most passionate and experienced Italian Communists, Rossana Rossanda, wryly commented, "reading a Red Brigades manifesto is like leafing through an old family album."

I thought I was reporting a commonplace, but there were people in the State Department and the CIA who went around town saying it was nonsense, and that in fact I was part of their very own propaganda effort to discredit the Soviets.

A couple of years later, when Khomeini was on the verge of seizing power in Iran, I and two other journalists—Judith Miller from *The New York Times* and

Steven Rosenfeld at the *Washington Post*—obtained translations of some of Khomeini's speeches and writings. We were all alarmed to discover that Khomeini was the ultimate counterrevolutionary, a vicious anti-Semite, and an intense anti-American, and that he intended to drag Iran back to a society he imagined had existed many centuries ago. Senator Henry "Scoop" Jackson shared our concerns, and he asked CIA Iran experts to enlighten him on the matter in 1979, just months before Khomeini seized power. They said they believed the documents we had cited were forgeries put out by the Israeli Mossad.

There are only two possibilities: Either they believed the nonsense they spoke, or they were lying to Congress and to their executive branch bosses. In either case, the country was badly served, yet there is good reason to believe that they knew the truth and preferred to please their customers at the State Department and the White House (or, if you wish to take a harsher view, that they had a political agenda to advance, and manipulated the intelligence to support their policy). President Carter and Secretary of State Vance had been very critical of the shah, and many other top officials in the Carter administration took a benevolent view of the anti-shah movement.

The Escape From the Truth

Robert Baer, whom my colleague Reuel Gerecht calls "one of the most talented Middle East case officers of the past twenty years (and the only CIA operative in the 1980s to collect consistently first-rate intelligence on the Lebanese Hizbollah and the Palestinian Islamic Jihad),"[7] spent nearly fifteen years trying to establish who had bombed the American embassy in Beirut in 1983. Despite the dimensions of the catastrophe and the seeming urgency to solve the mystery, the CIA seemed to lack the crucial information. But Baer finally got there: "In my last months (at the CIA)," he tells us, "I unraveled the . . . bombing, at least to my satisfaction: Iran ordered it, and a Fatah network carried it out."[8] It was the old Khomeini-Arafat partnership in action.

Baer's exhaustive researches went far beyond the Beirut mystery. In the process he also learned a chilling fact about the CIA itself.

It was clear from the documents I dredged up that, by at least 1997, the CIA knew the (Iranian) Pasdaran's command structure inside and out, just as it knew that Ayatollah Ali Khamene'i and President Rafsanjani approved every terrorist operation to come out of Iran. As I looked at the evidence in front of me, the conclusion was unavoidable: The Islamic Republic of Iran had declared a secret war against the United States, and the United States had chosen to ignore it.[9]

In short, the evidence was there, but several administrations didn't want to make too much of it. We knew that Hizbollah, under orders from Tehran, had blown up the Embassy (the PLO's role was not known at the time), but nobody was prepared to do anything about it. Ronald Reagan was not going to go to war against Iran; the Soviet Empire was enough.

Remember the intimate relationship between intelligence and policy: If the policy makers make it clear that they will not act on the basis of intelligence, then the intelligence pool eventually dries up. Without a clear national mission set by the president, even the best intelligence organization will perform poorly, because its work will lack focus and its case officers and analysts will avoid taking risks that cannot lead to rewards and advancement and might instead provoke official reprimands.

Just as the Congressional investigations into the FBI paralyzed initiative and candor within the Bureau, the Iran–Contra investigations stifled independent analysis at the Agency. Look at the list of the Agency officials who were fired in the wake of Iran–

Contra, and you'll find some of the best case officers in recent history. Look at the men who were promoted, and you'll find skilled bureaucrats who wrote politically acceptable reports, ignored "controversial" information, and never look a chance.

Over time, the lessons learned from the downfall of aggressive intelligence officers became part of the Agency's political culture. As Tom Powers, one of America's best students of the intelligence community, neatly sums it up, "A year in some country where it was dangerous to drink the water would get you no farther up the ladder than a year pushing paper in Langley."

Bill Casey was the last director of Central Intelligence with the will and wisdom—and the full support of his president—to drive the Agency to take the risks required to obtain first-class information about our enemies' intentions. Once he was gone, the CIA never had a chance to excel. Post-Casey directors were either cautious to the point of impotence, or severely weakened by the lack of an intimate working relationship with the White House. President George H. W. Bush was a supporter of the intelligence community (and was rewarded by having his name attached to the Agency's Virginia headquarters), but he placed the intelligence community under the inattentive eye of Judge William Webster, an honorable man with a severely limited understanding of world affairs, remarkably low energy, and no inclination to incur Congressional criticism. Webster bought Congressional favor by firing some of Casey's favorite officers, and he then studiously avoided doing anything to attract attention. After four years of treading water, the tempo of the CIA's decline resumed under Clinton.

The Final Straws

The two most devastating blows to a national intelligence service are penetration by its enemies and indifference from its leaders. Both struck the CIA in the first year of Clinton's presidency.

First came the terrible discovery that Aldrich Ames, a top official in the Soviet Division, had been secretly serving the KGB. And Ames was not the only Soviet "mole"; there was another KGB agent in the Operations Directorate named Harold Nicholson, and his discovery gave greater resonance to the crisis. Things got worse still with the emergence of yet another Soviet mole: Robert Hanssen, the head of FBI counterintelligence.

The discovery that Soviet moles had been at work at the highest levels of the American intelligence community had particular importance in our efforts to combat the terror masters. Agency analysts had long insisted that there was no conclusive evidence of Soviet involvement in international terrorism. One now had to wonder if that conclusion had been fed to us through the KGB moles in our midst. The KGB had long known what we knew about their activities, and men like Ames, Hanssen, and Nicholson were in a position to deflect our attention from information that pointed to Soviet involvement in the terror network, and manufacture information that indicated Soviet innocence.

At the same time that the intelligence community was reeling from the discovery it had been penetrated at very high levels, it soon became evident that Clinton had no interest in intelligence matters. His first DCI, James Woolsey, was a man of high intellect and impeccable character. But Woolsey was permitted no personal relationship with the president, and was no doubt astonished to discover that the president didn't want to talk to him. In two years on the job at Langley, Woolsey managed exactly two private conversations with Clinton, a record for futility. CIA career officers were quick to realize they'd been cut out of the action. When a thrill-seeker crashed his small plane on the South Lawn of the White House, the gag at the CIA was that it was probably Director Woolsey, desperately trying to find a way to get through to the president.

Faced with a combination of KGB moles and zero

access to the president, the CIA pulled in its horns and concentrated its energies on internal damage assessment. The CIA became so risk-averse that it shut its doors to Soviet-bloc defectors in Clinton's first year, thereby closing down one of the most useful sources of information on the terror masters. Thus, the Clinton administration failed to accept what the FBI later proclaimed "the most complete and extensive intelligence ever obtained from any source." Vasili Mitrokhin, who had been the chief archivist for the First Directorate of the KGB until 1985, had painstakingly hand-copied thousands of KGB documents, which he first offered to the CIA. When the Agency rejected him, he tried the British Secret Intelligence Service with greater success.

Mitrokhin's documents contained details on KGB foreign operations, including the identities of thousands of foreign agents—Western politicians, journalists, moviemakers, military officers, and diplomats. Some of them were still in positions of authority, others were retired and possibly willing to enlighten us on what they had done. In short, it was intelligence of the highest order, including information about Soviet connections to international terrorist organizations.[10]

It was a bad sign of the bad times. We couldn't trust our own people because they might be foreign agents, and the CIA couldn't recognize the proferred gift of the greatest intelligence find of all time. It's no surprise, then, that the intelligence community failed to notice that the terror masters in the Middle East were reorganizing their network. This was the gestation period for Al Qaeda, but we weren't much interested in the development of radical Islam in Afghanistan once the Red Army was defeated. A feisty Defense Intelligence Agency analyst by the name of Julie Sirrs was summarily dismissed when, despite formal approval from her agency, she traveled to the north of Afghanistan to see the legendary commander of the Northern Alliance, Ahmad Shah Massoud. And CIA headquarters rejected every request by Bob Baer to visit Massoud's territory.

CIA Director Woolsey quit in disgust after two years, and was followed by Deutch, the man who abandoned the Agency's basic mission. Deutch at least had a decent relationship with the president, but this was a mixed blessing at best; the CIA had greater input at the White House, but there was also far greater political influence over the Agency. Deutch imposed a heavy layer of political correctness on the intelligence community. All top officials were required to take sensitivity training and AIDS awareness courses, and the old Stansfield Turner model— the Agency as representative of the full diversity of the American people, quota by quota—was revved up again, with the usual bad results.

. . . In recent years the match between station chief and country got ever more arbi-
trary; one recent chief in Beijing . . . picked
for the job by Deutch's executive director,
Nora Slatkin, spoke no Chinese and suffered
from a conspicuous skin disease which the
Chinese find particularly offensive.[11]

This sort of thing was galling to the remaining professionals, and they were further enraged when
Deutch took the extraordinary step of appointing as
chief of operations a man who had spent his entire
career as an analyst, and had never run an agent in
his life. No such person, no matter how talented,
could hope to have the respect of experienced case
officers. The final insult was Deutch's open contempt
for the discipline of spycraft. He took home highly
sensitive information—including all current covert
actions—in his laptop computer, and then logged on
to the Internet, thereby exposing some of the country's most valuable secrets to anyone quick-witted
enough to hack in. Our enemies didn't have to go to
all the trouble of penetrating the CIA; the director
himself exposed our secrets to any skilled Internet
user. Predictably, there was a rapidly increasing loss
of experienced people who were not interested in
serving time at what was increasingly the Virginia
branch of the Department of State.

Following the example of the director, others began to publicly reveal sensitive information, often with damaging consequences. When Osama bin Laden moved to Afghanistan in 1996 he got a satellite phone, and we got the number. For two years we were able to secretly monitor and decrypt his phone calls. Then, in 1998, someone bragged about it to a journalist, the story was published, and bin Laden changed his phones, and his behavior. The intelligence community was confident bin Laden was in eastern Afghanistan in January 2002, because we had intercepted one of his phone calls from that region. But by that time Osama had known for nearly two years that we were listening to his calls. In all likelihood that intercepted "phone call" was a deception, a taped message transmitted from a place very far from bin Laden's true location.

As usual, the final blow came from Capitol Hill. In 1995, Congressman Robert Torricelli, vigorously abetted by enthusiasts in the media, mounted yet another scandal. Torricelli revealed that a CIA case officer in Guatemala had paid an informant who had been involved in violence in the past, apparently including the execution of a local guerrilla leader who was romantically involved with an American woman. It was the CIA equivalent of the FBI's Central American scandal a decade earlier (described in the last chapter). Both times the accusations were grossly inflated. Neither intelligence agency had broken the law. Both were engaged in proper activities that were necessary to advance our national security.

Any Director of Central Intelligence worthy of the name would have challenged Torricelli, because the congressman's accusations went to the very heart of the Agency's proper mission, especially in the war against terrorism. The question is whether our intelligence agencies should associate with unsavory characters, and the answer is, hell yes; that's why we have intelligence agencies in the first place. We have diplomats to deal with nice people, and spies and case officers for the others. If the CIA isn't permitted to recruit agents among the world's killers, it will inevitably fail to obtain firsthand information on the terror masters, all of whom are serial murderers.

But the Clinton Administration gave up on intelligence to look good on human rights. CIA Director Deutch admitted guilt where none existed, case officers were reprimanded, and new guidelines were drafted that tightened the restrictions on recruiting agents with dubious human rights records. While it was still theoretically possible to do it—the usual legalese stipulated that in exceptionally important cases, if you got formal approval from on high, you could chance such a recruitment—no case officer in his right mind would continue to pursue that kind of soiled-hands target.

No intelligence service could have kept its esprit de corps throughout the series of catastrophes that bludgeoned the CIA into grogginess by the time we had to deal with Osama bin Laden and his global network. By September 11, as Dewey Clarridge put it in his typically dry way, the CIA had become a cross between the Post Office and the Department of Agriculture.

In one of those rare events that illuminate the real forces at work within the American political community, shortly after September 11 there were calls for an investigation into the intelligence failures that made possible the attacks on American soil. On February 17, 2002, a Democratic senator insisted on the creation of a formal board of inquiry, to "help us understand the problems in our intelligence agencies and allow us to focus our resources more effectively."[12] The Senator was Robert Torricelli, the moving force behind the scandal that had led to the crippling guidelines. Torricelli evidently had no qualms about calling for an investigation that, if properly conducted, would unerringly identify him as one of the principal causes of the debacle.

Self-Destruction

Not all the damage was done by outside forces. There were additional wounds, some gratuitously and foolishly inflicted by years of poor management and shortsightedness by intelligence community officials, others flowing from the past missions that the CIA and the other components of the community had been ordered to perform for more than half a century.

The CIA was built to fight Soviet Communism and help win the Cold War. For half a century our main targets were KGB officers and their agents, not mullahs and sheikhs, let alone students in radical mosques or theological schools.

The Middle East was viewed in the context of the anti-Communist struggle, not as a problem unto itself. We wanted to prevent the Soviets from expanding their influence at the same time we expanded ours. There was no need for us to burrow deep inside the mysteries of the region; that was for the academics—and it is why you're more likely to understand Middle East terrorism from scholars like V. S. Naipaul, Bernard Lewis, or Fouad Ajami, or from disillusioned former CIA officers like Bob Baer and Reuel Gerecht, than from current Director George Tenet or his Middle East specialists. True, the CIA attracted some eccentric romantics who loved the Middle East and threw themselves into its cultures with great passion, but these were few and far between. And more often than not, the specialists were either the wrong sort of people, or their activities were so restricted by excessive bureaucratic concerns for their security and comfort that they were ineffective.

To penetrate a terrorist cell, you need a fluent Arabic or Farsi speaker who looks like he belongs, and you have to be willing to send him out there with no obvious link to the United States of America. He's got to have a credible (albeit false) biography (and this is tough in a part of the world where the family is the basic unit of society, because you've got to fabricate the man's entire family tree as well), and he has to operate on his own. The CIA lacks such people, and is unwilling to run the risks.

Reuel Gerecht, who spent nine years in the Operations Directorate targeting the Middle East, recalls that the Agency wouldn't send a lone officer to meet with a *possibly* dangerous foreigner,[13] and as for sending a genuine undercover agent into the field to blend in with the terrorists, Gerecht quotes a retired CIA officer:

> The CIA probably doesn't have a single truly qualified Arabic-speaking officer of Middle Eastern background who can play a believable Muslim fundamentalist who would volunteer to spend years of his life with shitty food and no women in the mountains of Afghanistan. For Christ's sake, most case officers live in the suburbs of Virginia. We don't do that kind of thing.

The finishing touch comes from another case officer: "Operations that include diarrhea as a way of life don't happen."

The failure to have such people and the unwillingness to order such missions are truly monumental and represent the deliberate subversion of the mission of the intelligence community. And while these failures have now focused public attention on the narrow field of counterterrorism, it can be assumed that we have similarly blinded ourselves in other areas.

Even so, even with the long history of decay and incompetence, even with the desire *not* to know too much about the terror masters, our leaders still had their chances. If they had behaved well we could have known enough about Al Qaeda and the terror network to have thwarted its evil designs. September 11 was indeed an intelligence failure, one of the worst in our history, but it also stemmed from a monumental failure of political leadership.

Every country in the world knows that the United States can determine its future, and no matter how many times American presidents fail to act decisively, foreign leaders—especially from small and middling countries who cannot guarantee their own survival—come to us for crucial assistance. We think of Osama bin Laden as a threat to America and Americans. True enough; but Al Qaeda could never bring down the United States. The terror master might, however, seriously threaten Islamic regimes in the Middle East, and those regimes had enough information on bin Laden to enable us to do away with him. That is why, in Clinton's second term, we had at least three exceptional opportunities to join with Arab leaders to take bin Laden out of action.

"The Biggest Mistake of my Presidency"

Dewey Clarridge's operation against Abu Nidal started with the terrorists' cash flow, both because it was the central nervous system of the organization and because it led the Counterterrorist Center investigators to the terrorists' partners, whether they were legitimate businesses or secret intelligence services. CIA got a full picture: The business side of Abu Nidal was run by a businessman in Warsaw, Poland, with the very un-Polish name of Samir Hasan Naim al-Din. Al-Din was an arms dealer, and his various companies moved weapons (for their own business and terrorist purposes and also to other groups and terror states like Syria, Iraq, and Libya), generated income for the group, and provided cover for Soviet-bloc intelligence services (primarily East Germany's Stasi and of course the Polish service).

Naim al-Din's financial network was the key to unraveling the Abu Nidal organization because almost everyone involved with the master terrorist dealt with money sooner or later. If the CIA could wreck al-Din's operations, we'd automatically devastate Abu Nidal. In like manner, bin Laden's financial network is the key to Al Qaeda, and the strength and global reach of the financial network demonstrates the urgency of going after him. By 1996 the State Department knew enough to brand him the number-one terrorist financier on earth. So we certainly had sufficient grounds to go after him with everything at our disposal.

As she so often does, Fortune offered the United States a golden opportunity in the mid-nineties, when President Bashir, the leader of Sudan's Islamic regime, approached Clinton with a fabulous offer. Sudan was on our official terrorist list, and we had imposed trade sanctions on Khartoum, which took a heavy toll on that nation's economy. The Sudanese hated being branded as pariahs, and they struggled to get out from beneath its stigma. As early as 1991 an American had been asked by a high-ranking Sudanese official to convey an offer (flatly rejected by Secretary of State James Baker) of full cooperation in the war against terrorism in exchange for a normal relationship. The Sudanese kept on trying with the next administration, and they used a Pakistani-American businessman, Mansoor Ijaz, who was a substantial contributor to the Clinton reelection campaign in 1996. In midsummer, Ijaz met with Sandy Berger and President Clinton, to whom he brought Bashir's offer to either keep bin Laden under close observation—specifically promising a gold mine of information on bin Laden's close working relationships with Hizbollah and Hamas—or turn him over to American authorities via Saudi Arabia.

Such offers are always suspect, but Sudan had a track record for betraying terrorists who were wanted men in the West. Less than two years earlier they had delivered to French security officers one of the world's most famous killers, the Venezuelan terrorist "Carlos the Jackal." The French locked him away in a Parisian jail cell for murdering French policemen a decade before. If the Sudanese could do it for the French, they could probably do it for us, too.

Moreover, the Sudanese had also pursued the matter through several diplomatic channels, both directly to our representatives, and indirectly through third countries. For example, Foreign Minister Ali Othman Taba asked our ambassador to Khartoum, Tim Carney, what Sudan could do to get itself off the terrorist list, and Carney diligently provided a menu, including closing the terrorist camps, expelling Egyptian terrorists (by then they had tried to assassinate Mubarak), and shutting down Osama. The Sudanese agreed, and the two options concerning bin Laden— extradition or close surveillance—were brought to Washington in March 1996, by Defense Minister Major-General Elatih Erwa. So the Clinton administration heard the same story through three channels, once from the Sudanese president, once from the foreign minister, and once from the defense minister.

The Saudis were understandably very nervous about putting their hands on their country's most celebrated black sheep. Everything about Osama made them upset. He was a member of one of the kingdom's most important families, and he thus benefited from a certain degree of protection from the royal family. On the other hand, the Saudis were one of bin Laden's prime rhetorical targets (even though, so far as I am aware, Al Qaeda has rarely taken any action against a Saudi target, or acted against a foreign target inside Saudi Arabia, and bin Laden has vigorously insisted that the nation's oil reserves are an invaluable treasure for the Islamic cause and should not be targeted by fellow terrorists). Also, they would have been reluctant to participate in anything that might lead to Osama's arrest or death. If they were to cooperate, the Saudis would require firm American guarantees that their footprints did not appear, and that we would act decisively against the entire operation. Opportunity had knocked, but Clinton and his national security team needed to show a lot of nerve before he could open the door.

They didn't have it, and they repeatedly rejected the Sudanese offers. After initial denials when the story came out after September 11, they explained their failure of nerve by resorting to the usual legal-

isms: Since we didn't have iron-clad proof of bin
Laden's guilt, we didn't ask for extradition, fearing
the significant embarrassment of a failed court case.[14]
Among those strongly opposed to arresting bin Laden
was FBI director Louis Freeh, who pointed out that
you can't use terrorists' confessions as evidence in domestic trials unless the sources themselves agree to
testify. A good deal of our evidence was of that nature, and thus, according to Freeh, unusable.

Freeh's position was typical, one might even say a
caricature, of the approach top U.S. administration
officials have taken in recent years. Someone determined to take the fight to the terrorists would have
argued quite differently. He would have pointed out
that the terrorists are waging war against us—the earlier 1993 World Trade Center conspiracy was sufficient to prove that—and are therefore subject to the
laws of war, as George W. Bush correctly asserted.
And the laws of war permit "anticipatory self-
defense."

> It is anticipatory self-defense . . . to cut off
> the bankroll that underwrites and replen-
> ishes terrorist networks. Even domestic law
> condemns individuals who aid and abet
> crimes, as well as those who "induce" crim-
> inal activities. Under the law of conspiracy,
> a sponsor is liable for ongoing criminal acts,

whether or not he knows of a particular target, so long as he knows the general nature of the enterprise. In March 1996, bin Laden clearly fulfilled these requirements.[15]

The Clinton administration didn't really want to take on the terrorists, and so they looked for legalistic justifications for inaction. If the administration had had the will to go after them, there were plenty of perfectly legal hooks on which to hang their policy hats.

Instead of pursuing one of our archenemies, we asked Bashir to expel bin Laden. Ever eager to please us, the Sudanese obliged. Bin Laden moved on to Jalalabad, along with a substantial and distinctly unsavory crowd: Ayman al-Zawahiri—the apparent mastermind of the September 11 attacks—Mamdouh Mahmud Salim—who got electronic gear for Al Qaeda in Europe—Wadih El-Hage—an American who served as bin Laden's personal secretary, now in jail for participating in the U.S. embassy bombings in Africa in 1998—and Fazul Abdullah Mohammed and Saif Adel, both accused of complicity in the embassy attacks.

The bombing of Khobar Towers, the U.S. military housing facility in Saudi Arabia, took place a scant month later. There was never any convincing evidence of Osama's involvement—everything pointed to the Iranians—but it should have raised our concern about terrorists nonetheless.

Whereupon our government's behavior got even worse. Early the following year—1997—with Osama installed in Afghanistan, the Sudanese were still eager to curry favor with us and they offered a considerable file of information on bin Laden in exchange for some improvement in relations. Clinton declined again. Then, in April, all conditions were removed from the Sudanese offer: no strings attached, just a present from one government to another. We again declined. Then the Sudanese offered the same files to the British government. The Military Intelligence Service, MI-6, was eager to read the material, but we intervened to prevent the transfer. It was not until the autumn of 2001 that the FBI, with a new director, a new attorney general, and a new president in office, finally obtained the bin Laden files from Sudan.

Clinton later told some friends that he considered this the worst mistake of his presidency, but his remark was both opportunistic (coming as it did after September 11) and insufficient (he has yet to explain why). There's a lot to explain. Why was the American government so desperately anxious that the Sudanese information on bin Laden *not* be consulted, either by our own counterterrorist experts or by those of Great Britain? The potential upside is easy to see—we might actually learn something important about a very dangerous person who was responsible for the murders of scores of Americans. What was the possible downside? Even if *we* didn't want to accept a favor from the Sudanese (aside from expelling him to Afghanistan), why on earth were we bound and determined that a friendly government, the British, not accept the information?

Reliable people give three kinds of explanation. The first has to do with the nature of Sudan. The Khartoum regime was an international pariah because of the regime's vicious Islamic campaign against the southern Christians and animists, and also because of the ongoing slave trade. One might argue that this was actually an argument in favor of getting involved, hoping to end the slavery and to mitigate the killing, but the Clinton people thought that the example of South Africa showed that we could encourage change by stigmatizing a government.

The second explanation is political: Osama might be a black sheep, but he was still a Saudi, and the Saudis were gun-shy about terrorism in general, and near-phobic about bin Laden. They almost certainly had more ties with him than they let on, both at the level of government and within the bin Laden family (which let it be known they had cut off Osama, while quietly helping him out when he was in need). We didn't want problems with Saudi Arabia that might threaten the booming American economy.

The third explanation is even more narrowly political, and applies to the entire terrorism issue: A vigorous counterterrorist campaign against bin Laden might have split the Democratic Party. The Democrat left wing, such as the apologists for Elijah Muhammed and others who embraced the Black Muslims' attacks on America as a racist and anti-Islamic society, would fight it. They'd say bin Laden just wasn't worth it. What did we think he'd done, as of early 1996? We did not know that Ramsey Yousef, the evil genius behind the 1993 World Trade Center bombing, had spent time in an Al Qaeda facility in Pakistan. Bin Laden claims that his fighters were involved in the Somalia campaign against United States troops, but we had no convincing proof of that. We probably suspected that he was behind the bombing of a Movenpick hotel in Aden, and a military facility in Riyadh, both in 1992, but the consequences were not substantial enough to get our undivided attention. His dramatic successes—from the embassy bombings to the attack on the U.S.S. *Cole*, to September 11—were still to come.

Each of these undoubtedly played a role, but the Clinton administration's compulsive desire *not* to know—because knowing would have demanded action, and Clinton wasn't prepared to act—lies at the heart of the matter. For the matter didn't end there. In the summer of 1998, just a few days before the embassy bombings, the Sudanese noticed two suspicious Arabs arrive on a flight from Nairobi. They gave a bin Laden manufacturing facility as their Sudanese address, and then rented a flat overlooking the (closed) American embassy. When the bombs exploded in Nairobi and Dar es Salaam, the Sudanese added two and two and got a jackpot: They arrested the two Arabs and accused them of being the Al Qaeda couriers who had carried the money from Afghanistan to the local terrorists in Kenya and Tanzania. The men confessed immediately, and the Sudanese promptly contacted the FBI and offered the men, the confessions, everything. The FBI was desperate to fly to Khartoum and lay their hands on the evidence, but once again they were restrained by the White House. When direct contacts failed to unblock the situation, the Sudanese sent a back channel directly to Washington to talk to one of the top people at the FBI's Counterterrorist Center, and this time the Bureau argued so violently for a meeting that it appeared we would finally get the culprits and the transcripts of their interrogations. But just as they were about to go to Khartoum, the FBI agents were told by the White House to step down. We were about to bomb the pharmaceutical firm in Khartoum, believing or pretending that it was a chemical weapons facility.

The Sudanese were so enraged that they released the two couriers, who sped back to Al Qaeda's home base in Afghanistan. Some months later the Sudanese calmed down, and once again offered us the interrogation transcripts. And once again the Clinton administration refused them. This time, the Clinton administration leaders could hardly claim that Osama wasn't worth our attention; he'd just killed hundreds of people on official American turf: the U.S. embassies in Kenya and Tanzania.

Whatever the explanation, Clinton's repeated refusals to even learn the full dimensions of the terrorist threat to the United States were unforgivable. To invert Talleyrand's famous condemnation of one of Napoleon's biggest missteps, it was worse than a blunder, it was a crime.

Clinton was not only not interested in action—demanding information about Al Qaeda—he was not interested in bin Laden himself. Monsoor Ijaz approached the White House again—this time meeting with Chief of Staff John Podesta—in July 2000, carrying a message from "a senior counterterrorism official from one of the United States' closest Arab allies" offering to lure bin Laden to that country and then turn him over to the U.S. There was a price (this is the Middle East, after all): a state visit during which Clinton would have to ask for bin Laden. Once again, the national security team debated the matter—by now bin Laden's importance had increased—and decided to check if the story was true. The traditional way to have done it would have been to discreetly approach the intelligence official for confirmation, but the White House chose a method guaranteed to torpedo the initiative. A top NSC official was dispatched to ask the country's ruler point-blank if the proposal was for real. Lacking a U.S. promise of the state visit, he promptly denied it, and that was that. Once again, Clinton had acted to guarantee failure.

Finally, there was an approach from yet another country in the region, perhaps Saudi Arabia, as usual from an intelligence officer. According to the London *Sunday Times*, "by one account, (the Saudis) offered to help place a tracking device in the luggage of bin Laden's mother, who was seeking to make a trip to Afghanistan to see her son. The CIA did not take up the offer."[16]

Clinton didn't even want to act against a different terror master, one who had tried to murder an American ex-president, who had used weapons of mass destruction against his own people, and who had been involved in the World Trade Center bombing of 1993: Saddam Hussein.

Saddam

Had we wanted to know about Al Qaeda's Sudanese years, we could easily have discovered many valuable things, including the close working relationship between bin Laden, Iran, and Iraq. This had been declared an impossibility by the CIA (part of the Shi'ites-don't-cooperate-with-Sunnis mantra), but, like the bumblebee that flies in violation of the laws of aerodynamics, the Iranian and Iraqi intelligence services worked closely with one another in cahoots with Al Qaeda and in violation of the CIA's conventional wisdom.

Unlike Al Qaeda, Iraq had become very prominent on our horizon, and for good reason. The Ba'ath (Arab Socialist) Party seized power in a coup in mid-1968, and over the next eleven years Saddam Hussein gradually amassed enough power to proclaim himself president. In June–July 1979, immediately after his seizure of power, Saddam purged five hundred top Ba'ath Party officials, a tribute to both his ruthlessness and his care in identifying unreliable persons. His home base secured, he turned his ambitious gaze outward and attacked Iran, then riven by chaos and internal strife following Khomeini's triumphal revolution.

Saddam's reign has been one of the bloodiest in the region. The war with Iran cost roughly a million

Iraqi lives, but Saddam had enough energy left over to slaughter nearly two hundred thousand Kurds in 1988, many of them killed by poison gas. His invasion of Kuwait in 1991 provoked the Gulf War, and another scourge of death and misery.

Despite this catalogue of horror, Saddam, prior to the invasion of Kuwait, was generally viewed with respect and sometimes even admiration by the Western diplomatic establishment, which saw his secular movement as a counterforce to Khomeini's lunatic fundamentalism. Fouad Ajami summarized Saddam's attractiveness to the west as: "You wear pants, I wear pants." Plus, he had oil, always good for relations with the industrialized countries. It was not until the Gulf War that Saddam was transformed from rational Arab statesman to fiendish mass murderer (considerably more accurate), and so he has remained.

The earlier Bush administration's failure to see the Gulf War through to its logical conclusion—the removal of Saddam's regime—must be counted as one of the major blunders of recent American foreign policy, and left us groping for another way to accomplish a meaningful conclusion. First we invited the northern Kurds and southern Shi'ites to rise up against Saddam, an invitation that normally implies willingness to support the insurrection, and it was so taken by the Iraqi people. The insurrection did indeed occur, shortly after the Gulf War cease-fire, but our support was only words not deeds, and Saddam had enough military power left after the Gulf War defeat to crush the insurgents.

Again trying to make the best of a bad situation, Bush the Elder created a "no fly" zone in the north, where the Kurds and some Shi'ites could take refuge. We fed them, provided blankets and clothing, and half-heartedly spoke of organizing new attempts to overthrow the dictator. This mission gained urgency after Saddam was caught plotting to assassinate former President Bush on a celebratory trip to Kuwait in 1993, but to no avail. One could fill a small volume with accounts of failed coup attempts—the CIA's method of choice—but suffice it to say that over time, hundreds of plotters and accomplices went to hideous deaths, and not one came close to succeeding. On some unfortunate occasions the Agency's incompetence bordered on buffoonery; in March 1996, the Agency's coup plotting was so easily detected that Saddam's security chief telephoned the CIA case officer on the covert communications system he'd given to the coup leaders, to say that the CIA's man had just been executed.

The idea of an insurrection did not die, however, and a rough coalition of Kurds and Shi'ites was cobbled together in the northern sanctuary by an unlikely Shi'ite businessman/intellectual named Ahmed Chalabi. There was never any question about Chalabi's smarts—anyone with a Ph.D. in mathematics from the University of Chicago has enough brains for most any undertaking—or about his standing (his family had been important in the politics of the region for hundreds of years). But many in the State Department and in the intelligence community doubted such an undertaking could succeed. The Kurds were famously divided, the Shi'ites were tainted with suspicions of Khomeinism, and Chalabi was very independent minded, which is invariably unpopular with CIA people, who like to think they're in charge. But Chalabi got results, and his Iraqi National Congress achieved a surprising degree of unity among the Kurds, as well as a manifest concern in Baghdad. He finally won a grudging acceptance from the CIA, and the INC designed an ambitious plan to overthrow Saddam by a combination of popular insurrection, military attack, and armed seizure of power.

At the eleventh hour the Clinton White House again lost its nerve, and called off the operation.[17] With everything falling apart, some members of the INC went ahead anyway, and scored some short-lived military successes. But with Washington in full retreat there was no chance to remove Saddam. Some months later, he sent his tanks north into the INC enclave. Clinton had warned that any attack from Baghdad would trigger a violent response, but Saddam called his bluff and won. Clinton did nothing. At one point, as Saddam's forces were slaughtering the opposition forces, American fighter pilots over the two battle zones, enraged at the spectacle of our allies being killed by the Iraqi Army, radioed back for permission to shoot down the helicopters and bomb the tanks. Permission was denied. Indeed, Clinton did worse: The CIA managed to rescue a remnant of the anti-Saddam forces and shipped them overseas (to Guam, for example). Then the Clinton Administration accused several of them of being Iraqi spies, and was on the verge of sending them to certain death in Iraq. Fortunately they found a top-notch defense lawyer: former CIA Director James Woolsey. Thanks to his access to classified material, the cases fell apart, and they were permitted to stay in the United States.

You have only to look at the history of the American response to Iraq to understand why the terror masters felt confident they could attack the United States and American allies with impunity on September 11. The first Bush administration had Saddam on the ropes, and declined to put him away. The Clinton administration botched a whole series of coup attempts, and then betrayed the one group that showed promise. And just as the American refusal to even obtain the facts about Osama bin Laden has continued for many years, the State Department and the CIA still fight furiously in order to avoid supporting the INC, even though Congress has appropriated tens of millions of dollars for just that purpose.

Consequences

Years of White House fecklessness produced disastrous consequences among those of our would-be allies and friends who command nations at serious risk. Their daily travail is devoted to survival, not to "politics." Such men and women do not have the luxury of friendly neighbors and protective oceans, or irresistible armies wielding devastating weapons. They have to deal with mortal threats to themselves and their nations, and they must judge whether, and to what extent, they should incur risks by advancing our interests.

Friendship with America makes you an enemy of America's enemies. If you help the United States destroy a terrorist network, you'd better be damn sure the network is truly destroyed, because it will surely come after you. So you always have to ask yourself if the Americans will stand by you, and for many years now, the answer has been "no way."

Even our powerful allies are full of misgivings, and have been for quite a while. In 1985 President Reagan sent the late General Vernon Walters to Paris to ask if American fighter-bombers could fly over France en route from England to Libya, where they would attack the terror regime of Muammar Qadaffi. The French president, François Mitterrand, and the prime minister, Jacques Chirac, asked Walters about the mission. Was it part of a strategy to overthrow Qadaffi? Or was it just one more American newspaper-headline gesture? Would we fight until Qadaffi was gone, or would we drop our bombs, fly back to England, and leave the French to deal with the consequences? Walters's answer would determine the French decision. If we were serious, then not only would France grant permission for the overflights, but they would join with us, and provide ground power. The French Foreign Legion was available, and it had tanks, planes, and good fighters. But if we were not serious, then it was best for us to take the long way around. When Walters informed the French that we only planned a single bombing attack and not a sustained operation to remove Qadaffi, we were forced to take the long route. It was another bit of evidence that the oft-proclaimed "war against terrorism"—then against Qadaffi—was more smoke than fire.

What's sauce for overflights is sauce for other forms of assistance, from political support to intelligence sharing. Many prudent leaders decided to wait and see, reasoning that there would be time enough to be a good friend when and if the Americans got serious. The Saudis, for example, paid close attention to the events of 1995 and 1996, when our proxies in Iraq were routed by Saddam Hussein. You can be certain that their refusal to cooperate with us on bin Laden was due at least in part to our defeat in Iraq.

On the other side of the barricades, our enemies took heart, and their ranks swelled. The year 1996 was not only the one in which Saddam struck against American interests in northern Iraq. It was the same year that Osama bin Laden relocated to Afghanistan, expanded his operations, and won important new allies. As the terror masters killed more and more of us, and our government's responses were few, feeble, and far between, they concluded that we were afraid or incapable of fighting. They looked at us and saw a country besotted with materialism and self-indulgence, led by men and women who dreaded the very idea of body bags. Their dreams and terror fantasies became ever more ambitious, until eventually they imagined that if they killed enough Americans, they could impose their will on us.

That is how we got September 11.

4

HOW TO WIN THE WAR

No people in history have ever survived who thought they could protect their freedom by making themselves inoffensive to their enemies.

—DEAN ACHESON AND PAUL NITZE

Our leaders and our country have three tasks:

- secure our homeland, a daunting undertaking in a country that prides itself on its openness and whose people have always felt secure and have always welcomed foreigners, especially those who claim to be fleeing oppression

- kill or incarcerate the terrorists, of whom the president has told us there are tens of thousands, with cells in at least sixty countries

- bring down the terror masters, the rulers of those regimes that provide the terror network with the critical infrastructure—training, safe havens, travel documents, technology and all the rest—they need to operate.

Our leaders have been at pains to insist that we are not engaged in a religious war, that Islam is a religion of peace, and that most Muslims disapprove of the terrorist onslaught. Yet the terror masters, from Iraq's Saddam Hussein and Syria's Bashar Assad to the Iranian ayatollahs and Osama bin Laden, all use the language of Islam to justify their actions and to recruit, train, and motivate the killers. Those who danced in the streets of the Middle East to celebrate September 11 did so in the name of Islam.

The best way to understand the role of Islam is to think back to World War III, our half-century struggle with the Soviet Empire.

Throughout the Cold War experts differed on the extent to which the Soviet Empire was a purely geopolitical threat or whether the ideology of communism was the central menace. Both were right. Like the blind men groping the elephant, each understood a piece of the puzzle. We certainly had to contend with the growth of Soviet military power, lest the Soviets be able to dictate terms to us from a position of strategic supremacy. But the Soviet Empire was also a revolutionary state, and most Soviet leaders believed they were the instruments of vast historical forces that guaranteed their ultimate victory over the capitalist West. Even Mikhail Gorbachev, the unwitting catalyst of the implosion of the Soviet Union, labored to the last to save Soviet communism. He never intended to abandon it, and he never foresaw its collapse.

We defeated the Soviet Empire both militarily and ideologically, and there was a dynamic interplay between the two. The communist leaders believed that history was on their side. This belief was codified in the so-called Brezhnev Doctrine, which said that once communism had been installed in a given country it could not be reversed. It was one more milestone on the road to the communist future. Accordingly, when countries that had been proclaimed communist, like Grenada and Afghanistan, ceased to be ruled by loyal comrades and left the Soviet bloc, a shock wave went through the entire Empire. The Brezhnev Doctrine was shown to be false, and this suggested that history had changed its course, giving heart to the anticommunists and undermining communist morale.

One form of power comes from the barrel of a gun, but another flows from the human spirit, and once communism had been defeated in one of its citadels, followers and leaders alike began to lose heart. Soviet leaders no longer saw themselves as the instruments of the inevitable flow of human history, and their opponents began to think of themselves as potential winners . . . along with us, and our revolutionary ideals of freedom and democracy.

Thoughtful American strategists saw from the beginning that we would have to defeat the Soviet Union at both levels, with superior military strength and superior ideals. The celebrated American philosopher of the Cold War, George F. Kennan of the State Department, foresaw in the late 1940s that if we could contain Soviet communism, it would eventually devour itself. Once it was apparent that its messianic mission had failed, the Soviet Empire could not endure, unless it could replace its failed worldview with brute power.

The same holds for the war against the terror masters, who have attacked us physically and ideologically. Radical Islam—what several commentators have called "Islamism" to stress its nontraditional ideological emphasis—is to this war what communism was to the Cold War. Like the Soviet Union, the terror states are both believers in a revolutionary doctrine and commanders of armies. Like the Soviets, the radical Islamists believe they have found the key to getting on the right side of history. Like the communists, they insist that their radical vision is the wave of the future (while, to be sure, simultaneously claiming that it was also the wave of the past, a notable difference). Like the Soviets, their mass appeal depends heavily on continuous success. Remember bin Laden's survey of recent events: defeat of the Soviets in Afghanistan, and humiliation of the Americans in Somalia, Lebanon, East Africa, New York, and Washington—all to show that his cause was just. If the tide of history turns visibly against him, bin Laden—alive or dead—will lose favor.

All losers are rejected by their former and would-be followers, and those who claim Divine authority, whether from Allah or the gods of history, are rejected even faster. Don't forget how quickly the Soviet Empire imploded, to the astonishment of most of the world. As the terror war progresses, we will be equally surprised at the speed with which the terror masters collapse. As they begin to lose, their people will turn on them, for most of their people are neither crazy nor stupid.

The terror network and the Soviet Empire have one other common feature: their tyrannical leaders. It is easy to oversimplify the war by describing it as a war with Islam, or a war with Islamic Arabs. But there are enormous religious and political differences among the terror masters. Some are Shi'ites, others are Sunni. Some, like Saddam Hussein and Hafez al-Assad, built their power on secular foundations and only embraced radical Islam when it became popular. Others are deeply religious, like bin Laden and Khomeini.

But the common denominator of the terror masters is tyranny. They are all dictators, whether, like the Iranian mullahs, they actually rule or whether, like Osama bin Laden, they aspire to it. As the communist dictators used Marxist-Leninist doctrine to justify their tyrannical rule, so Muslim leaders claim Divine Right to oppress their people. Osama bin Laden's jihad is supposed to lead to "the establishment of a castle of the Muslims, a (new) Caliphate," where mosque and state will merge in a transnational Nation of Islam.[1]

So while there are many peaceful Muslims, the terror masters follow a tyrannical and bellicose version of Islam.

This is why we are inescapably the bulls-eye in their target, for all tyrants and would-be tyrants fear and therefore hate America. Our great success threatens their legitimacy, for most of their own people would prefer to be free and would prefer to choose their own leaders. Usually they don't want the repressive rulers they have. So long as America flourishes, all tyrants are threatened. Sooner or later, they are impelled to come at us, desperate to demonstrate that their way is better, that we are weak, and that it is folly to challenge them.

The tyrants' hatred of America is not the result of any given American policy. It is our existence, not our actions, that threaten them, because our existence inspires their people to desire different rulers in a different kind of polity.

If it were simply a matter of our actions, the leaders of the Muslim world would hail America as one of the greatest allies they've ever had. Look at the amazing number of times the United States has sent soldiers, advisers, and hundreds of millions of dollars overseas to defend Muslim populations. We twice intervened in Afghanistan, first against the Red Army and then against the Taliban. We rescued Kuwaiti Muslims and defended Saudi Muslims from the depredations of Saddam Hussein, along with Northern Iraq's Kurdish and Shi'ite Muslims. We fought for Muslims against their Christian enemies in Bosnia and Kosovo. Without us, Osama bin Laden might well have fallen to atheist Soviet troops in Afghanistan. None of this wins us any admiration or gratitude, because our existence, rather than our policies, underlies the terror masters' rage against us.

Which is not to say that their rage is not Muslim rage, nor that they view their struggle with us as one between freedom and tyranny. Not at all; Osama is well and truly enraged at the presence of American troops on sacred Saudi sand, and many Middle Eastern leaders (not just the terror masters) are enraged at our support for Israel. But bin Laden only recently discovered the Palestinian cause, and Saddam only recently adopted Islamic discourse (while claiming to have always been a man of deep religious faith), just as he only recently let it be known that he had donated fifty pints of his own blood to produce the scarlet ink for a handwritten copy of the Koran in a mosque outside Baghdad. A scant fifteen years ago he was commonly portrayed as a hopeful example of a growing Arab secularism and as a political counterpoise to the kind of radical Islamism running amok next door in Iran. As for the Assads in Damascus, don't forget that Hafez needed Khomeini's blessing to acquire a grudging legitimacy from the Shi'ite faithful in Syria. His own instincts and beliefs, like those of Saddam, were secular and anti-Western: The Ba'ath movement was based on radical socialism.

The Cold War model also helps us understand the differences between our war with the Soviet Union and the war against terrorism. We defeated the Soviet Union after communism had visibly failed. Even the members of the Politburo were calling for dramatic reform, or *glasnost*. No Soviet leader would have dared to suggest that communism was failing because the Kremlin had drifted away from Lenin's original vision; the communists themselves knew that something new was required. The radical Islamists, however, blame the long decline of the Muslim world on the abandonment of the original faith, with the consequent corruption of Muslim leaders and the emasculation of Muslim energies. Western criticism of the failure of Muslim states in the Middle East and elsewhere does not strike at the core of the Islamists' vision, because they fully agree that many Muslim states are failures. Indeed, the visible shortcomings of the so-called "moderate Arab governments" are the starting point of their violent revolt.

We will therefore need to demonstrate that radical Islamism is a road to humiliation and defeat, not a pathway to glory. Our Cold War strategy of deterrence isn't likely to work. It's hard to deter suicide terrorists,[2] and during the past twenty years many terrorist organizations have used them. According to *Jane's Foreign Report*,[3] ten terrorist groups have developed suicide terrorism as a regular tactic: Hamas, the Palestinian Islamic Jihad, Hizbollah, the Egyptian Islamic Jihad (EIJ) and Gemaya Islamiya (Islamic Group—IG) of Egypt, the Armed Islamic Group (GIA) of Algeria, Barbar Khalsa International (BKI) in India, the Tamil Tigers in Sri Lanka (the only group to have killed two world leaders—the former prime minister of India, Rajiv Gandhi, and the president of Sri Lanka, Ranasinghe Premadasa—using male and female suicide bombers), the Kurdistan Worker's Party (PKK) of Turkey, and of course Al Qaeda.

Women have often been active in terrorist organizations (even at high levels; a woman staged the suicide assassination of Rajiv Gandhi), and there are several precedents (and solid operational reasons) for female kamikazes in the Middle East and South Asia. Several suicide operations in Lebanon were carried out by women, and three years ago Israeli authorities thwarted a planned Islamic Jihad operation that featured a female suicide bomber. Nearly a third of the suicide operations in Sri Lanka have been conducted by women. As *Jane's* noted, there are at least three good reasons for using women in terrorist operations: Security personnel are less suspicious of women; there is still a taboo against males performing extensive body searches of females; and women can conceal explosives under their clothes by dressing as if they were pregnant.

Our overall mission was defined early on by President Bush when he declared war on the terrorists themselves and on the countries that harbor or support terrorism—but it is complicated in practice. Each of the terror masters requires a different line of attack. Some, like Saudi Arabia, will be very difficult, while others, like Iran, will be surprisingly easy. The Iranian people are overwhelmingly on our side. They have repeatedly demonstrated their disgust with the dominant theocracy and can be expected to vigorously attack the regime once it is clear we have targeted the ruling mullahs and ayatollahs. Many important Saudis, on the other hand, seem to be true believers in the Islamist doctrines of the kingdom, and while there is considerable economic discontent there are no signs of rebellion against the royal family or against the Wahhabi establishment. Iraq is more similar to Iran than to Saudi Arabia, and Saddam Hussein probably does not have great popular support. Neither does Bashar Assad in Syria.

We have an understandable tendency to overrate the terrorists and underrate ourselves, as so many did prior to the Gulf War and again before the fighting started in Afghanistan. The speed with which Al Qaeda and the Taliban collapsed in the face of our attacks suggests that we're not exactly up against Caesar's finest legions.

We are also likely to benefit from the blunders typical of the terror masters; sometimes they're both crazy *and* stupid. Years ago, some of Qadaffi's agents negotiated the purchase of surface-to-air missiles in Italy for an enormous sum of money. They sneaked into Rome to collect the missiles, loaded them onto a flatback truck, and headed south at such speed that they were stopped by the highway police. Something about the agents' behavior raised suspicion, and the police decided to open the packages in the truck. The packages turned out to contain telescopes. The Libyans had been ripped off.

The same thing happened to Osama in Afghanistan. In November 2001, the world press carried the alarming news that Western troops had found instructions for the construction of a nuclear bomb in an Al Qaeda safe house in Kabul. After careful analysis, the Internet newsletter rotten.com announced that the document in question had come from the *Journal of Irreproducible Results*, and was entitled "How To Build An Atomic Bomb In 10 Easy Steps." The bomb itself was described as "a great ice-breaker at parties, and in a pinch, can be used for national defence."[4] All of which caused the London *Telegraph*'s science editor to remark that the terrorist group, at least in this case, "had little idea what it was doing and absolutely no sense of humour."

On the other hand, there is no doubt that capable scientists were and are employed by Syria, Iran, and Iraq to help develop weapons of mass destruction. Despite repeated public and private guarantees from Russian leaders, it would be a pleasant surprise to learn that the terror masters did not purchase some of the Soviet inventory after the fall of communism. They must have grabbed some of it. So we musn't dawdle; but we also shouldn't permit ourselves to be overwhelmed with dread.

First and foremost, we must bring down the terror regimes, beginning with the big three: Iran, Iraq, and Syria. And then we have to come to grips with the Saudis.

Iran: Revolution From Within

A potentially world-historical event is underway in the largest and most powerful terrorist country of the Middle East, yet no one has noticed it for a long time. It could well mark the major turning point in the war against terrorism, for the fall of the Islamic Republic would be the current equivalent of the fall of the Soviet Union. Iran is the driving force behind international terrorism, and without Iran the terror network would be seriously weakened. Moreover, Iran established the kind of regime Osama dreams of, and its destruction would be as psychologically and ideologically devastating to the Islamists as, irony of ironies, the defeat of the Red Army in Afghanistan was to the communists.

The unraveling of the Islamic Republic has actually been underway for some time. Beginning the night of October 12, 2001, the citizens of Iran repeatedly demonstrated against the murderous Shi'ite theocracy. The October riots, which ran for four successive nights in Tehran and other major cities, were unprecedented in the history of the Islamic Republic. They involved hundreds of thousands of people at a minimum. One secondhand account I received spoke of more than a million anti-government demonstrators in Tehran alone.

Unlike previous demonstrations, which were largely limited to students at major universities, the latest round of violence involved people from all walks of life, men and women alike. And while all the riots started following international soccer matches involving the national team, they were clearly political. Demonstrators carried slogans attacking the Islamic regime and its leader, Ayatollah Ali Khamene'i. They chanted nationalist anthems, demanded political freedom, and hurled stones at the dreaded security forces. In an outright show of contempt for the guardians of the revolution, boys and girls danced in the streets, taunting the Islamic authorities. Thousands of young people were arrested (the regime admitted to more than two thousand), and countless others hospitalized. Detainees under eighteen were herded into special detention centers, while older ones faced judgment at the hands of the Islamic Revolutionary courts.

The country's leaders were visibly shaken, to the point where the minister of the interior was allegedly told to "fill all the hospital beds in the country." The mullahs seriously feared they were entering their final days in power.

The demonstrations first erupted following Iran's 1–0 defeat of Iraq on October 12. The following week, fearing new outbursts, the government apparently ordered the national team to throw its match against Bahrain, a no-account team. But when Iran lost 3–1, new riots ensued, this time supported by enraged fans. Then, on October 25, more demonstrations started after Iran beat the United Arab Emirates 1–0. Following those outbursts, the government responded by confiscating satellite dishes all over the country, a heavy-handed move that confirms that nobody believes the official "news."

These potentially earth-shaking revolutionary events in Iran escaped the notice of our top policy makers and our media until well into October. There was not a line on it in the newspapers during the two weeks following the initial demonstrations, and when one of our top foreign policy officials was asked whether we intended to support the young Iranians, he angrily replied, "Why have I heard nothing about this?"

He didn't know about it for the usual reasons. There was very little information from the intelligence community, and most of what there was tended to present a fairly positive picture of the regime. This dovetailed nicely with the State Department's desire to reach some sort of workable compromise with the Islamist tyrants. Indeed, in interagency meetings, top officials from Foggy Bottom

went so far as to claim that we had an "historic opportunity" to work with the Iranian government
throughout the region. When challenged, they admitted there were some nasty and even evil people
atop the regime, but argued that there were also
some good people, and we should help the good people thwart the bad guys.

The Iranian people—above all those who supported President Khatami and his so-called "reform-
ers"—do not suffer from these illusions. The Islamic
regime in Tehran has long since lost any semblance
of popular support, and it has maintained power only
through the systematic use of terror against its people. Surely it cannot claim popular support on the
basis of its accomplishments, because twenty-three
years of theocracy have produced ruin and misery.
Four million have fled the revolution, most of them
well educated and highly skilled. The data on those
trapped by the tyrants are startling:

- 60 percent of the population lives below the pov-
  erty line

- one-third to one-half of all Iranians are malnour-
  ished

- the average income for more than half the population is $1.40 per day

- the gross domestic product is less than half of what it was in 1978

- The distribution of the shrinking wealth is firmly in the hands of the regime, and inequitably allotted. More than 80 percent of the country's gross national product comes from the petroleum industry, which is entirely in government hands. The mullahs have effectively ruined this primary source of national wealth: Oil production is currently 3.2 million barrels per day. It was 6.2 at the end of the shah's rule

- Inflation has run wild. The exchange rate was seventy-two rials to the dollar in '78, and it is more than eight thousand today.

No wonder there are said to be more than fifty thousand suicides per year. And no wonder one of the regime's leading figures told the nation in early May 2002 that Iran's economy was at least as crippled as Argentina's.

Europeans shun the country. *Newsweek International* proclaimed Iran the "worst country in the world for journalists" in the summer of 2001, and the French-led international organization, *Reporters sans frontières*, branded Ayatollah Khamene'i one of the world's top enemies of a free press.

All of this might have been tolerated in the name of the true faith if the leaders had demonstrated a virtuous asceticism (as, for example, bin Laden does). But the regime is one of the most corrupt in memory, and the tyrant has instituted a unique form of state theft. A percentage of most business deals, and even many elementary cash transactions, is deposited in an account known as the "leadership's household," which is entirely at the disposal of the supreme leader, the Ayatollah Ali Khamene'i. If you buy a car—the national vehicle is the Peykan—the base price is roughly $6,250 but you have to pay $8,125. The difference goes to Khamene'i. Thus the leadership is awash in money while the people starve.

Those who protest are arrested, tortured, or executed. More than a hundred Iranians were assassinated in Europe, the United States, and the Middle East between 1979 and the beginning of 2001, in keeping with the straightforward pronouncement of Ahmad Janati, the secretary of the Council of Guardians (on June 15, 2001: "those opposing the regime must be killed"). Assassination is held in such regard that a street in Tehran was renamed after Khaled Islambouli, Anwar Sadat's killer.

It is therefore easy to understand why the street protesters are young; older persons are unlikely to challenge such a repressive regime. But the young are the majority in Iran—well over half the population is under twenty-five years of age, and they have shown themselves willing to take risks. Leaders of the student movement, which is one of the few centers of anti-regime thought and action, are routinely rounded up, thrown in jail, and tortured. This was done right after the October demonstrations, for example, and then again shortly after President Bush's "axis of evil" speech, when he branded Iran one of the terror states.

The regime is visibly nervous, since it knows its people would vote out the theocracy if they had a chance. Public opinion polls to the contrary notwithstanding, Iranian "elections" clearly demonstrate the public's real mood: More than 70 percent vote for the most "reformist" candidate available, President Khatami. They know that Khatami won't change anything (if he tried, he, too, would occupy a cell in the Evin Prison in Tehran), but a vote for Khatami is the only safe form of open protest available to them. Khatami is the empty vessel into which the Iranians have poured their rage against the regime. Those who doubt Khatami's emptiness should remind themselves that more than two hundred reformists were removed from the list of candidates by the dominant hardliners. He was judged one of the least offensive.

Censorship is as important to the Iranian regime as to any other tyranny, and the mullahs have shut down virtually every independent publication in the country—a further sign that they know they are hated. But there are still sources of accurate information, particularly from outside the country, and the Iranians listen to international radio and watch satellite television (above all, National Iranian TV, which broadcasts from Los Angeles to a big audience in Iran).

One of the apparent paradoxes of Middle East politics is that Islamic radicalism flourishes in countries with corrupt governments allied with the United States—like Saudia Arabia and Egypt—but is hated in an anti-American Islamist country like Iran. The Iranian people have been vaccinated against radical Islam; they have lived under its yoke for more than two decades, and they know its miseries all too well. That is why so many of them took to the streets following the September 11 attack on New York and Washington, carrying candles in silent support of the United States. If they succeed in freeing themselves from Iran's evil oppression, they will banish the mullahs to their mosques, hold a referendum that will almost surely create a secular republic, and ally themselves with us. As an Iranian friend once said to me, "If the Pakistanis, after the death of General Zia, could elect a secular woman president, imagine what we will do after the death of the mullahs."

This is a terrifying prospect for those who are advocating Islamism as a remedy for the ills of the Middle East, and for the centuries'-old decline of the Islamic world. If Iran falls, the people of the region will see that two Middle Eastern countries—one Sunni (Afghanistan), one Shi'ite (Iran)—installed Islamist regimes, and both went to their ruin accompanied by the enthusiastic rejection of their peoples. No wonder that several leading Iranian ayatollahs are now quietly calling for a quick end to the Islamic Republic. Some of the leading religious authorities have even begun to openly challenge the doctrines of the regime. In early May, the Grand Ayatollah Montazeri—the highest-ranking religious figure outside the regime, long under house arrest in the sacred city of Qom—issued a *fatwa* proclaiming that suicide terrorism was a heresy, and those who encouraged it were committing a sin. Religious leaders like the Ayatollah Montazeri fear that if things continue as they are, Islam itself will go down along with the theocracy. They know that the Iranian people do not want more Islam; they want more freedom.

It is hard to imagine a greater triumph for our war against the terror masters than a successful popular uprising against the regime of the Islamic Republic. It follows that we must encourage it and then support the new government.

President Bush took the first step when he denounced the Islamic Republic as a self-appointed elite that represses the Iranian people's desire for freedom. It was an important step, not least of all because it delivered a stern rebuff to those in the State Department who had convinced themselves that we could craft an alliance with the "moderates" within the Iranian government, and work with them to defeat terrorism and stabilize Afghanistan after the fighting. Bush understood that bringing Iran into an antiterrorist alliance was akin to inviting Communist Bulgaria into NATO at the height of the Cold War, and that whatever the desires of the so-called moderates in Tehran, they were powerless. Furthermore, the Iranian regime does not want a stable Afghanistan, and above all it does not want a successful Afghanistan in which someone with the title of "shah," or king, plays a role, as this might prompt the Iranians to support a return to monarchy in their own country.

But the president's strong words led most people in the region to believe that he would soon order strong actions, and these, alas, did not follow. For many long weeks there was no follow-up, even in word, thereby leaving the pro-American Iranians in the worst possible position. The regime interpreted Bush's statement as a declaration of war, and set about defending itself. More than forty student leaders were rounded up and imprisoned. Censorship was tightened even further. The various instruments of repression, from the Revolutionary Guards to the secret police, were put on heightened alert, and—just to show how frightened they were—emergency consultations were held with the governments of Syria, Iraq, and North Korea to plan mutual assistance when the American attack came.

We should have been ready, at a minimum, to step up our declarations in support of freedom-loving Iranians. Top administration officials might have attacked the repressive steps taken by the mullahs. The single statement followed by inertia conjured up images of Father Bush's abandonment of the Iraqis when they attempted to overthrow Saddam at the end of the Gulf War. Secretary of State Powell seemed to have no stomach for a steady assault on the evils of the Iranian regime, and even let it be known that he still hoped that some kind of "diplomatic solution" could be found. It was not until the middle of March that the National Security Council's Zalmay Khalizhad forcefully presented the long list of Iranian evildoing to an Iranian–American audience in Washington.

Freedom is our most powerful weapon, and the Iranian people are our greatest asset against the mullahs. We need to be more considerate of their fate. They need to hear and see that we are with them and they also need to see that we are prepared to act. At the same time we denounce the regime, we should demand the release of the student leaders, teachers, and journalists, and call for free expression and freedom of the press. And we should increase direct radio and television broadcasting to Iran through the Voice of America, Radio Liberty, and Radio Free Europe, and also through the various private broadcasters such as Iranian National TV in Los Angeles.

At the same time, we must find ways to support the opposition. This is not as difficult as might be imagined. There are several Iranian networks in Europe and the United States, and by now we know which ones are reliable and can funnel assistance to the Iranian dissidents, and which are fronts for the regime. The people inside Iran will need modest financial support, and perhaps some guidance on how to strengthen their nonviolent movement. If it is possible to get them advance notice concerning our public policy, they will be able to coordinate their actions with our public statements.

It will be objected that the regime is prepared to fight, and that violence will inevitably be required to bring it down. In truth, nobody knows that that's the case, not even the mullahs themselves. Several communist regimes fell in the face of concerted public demonstrations of contempt, and even their dreaded secret police lost their nerve and went over to the side of freedom. The Revolutionary Guards and the *Basiji* have proven themselves capable of killing off dissidents one by one in the torture chambers of Evin

Prison in Tehran, but it is a different matter when you have to face a great mass of unarmed fellow countrymen and countrywomen. Look at Slobodan Milosevic, a mass murderer who went quietly after it became clear he was detested by his own people. Or consider the case of General Jaruzelski in Poland, who was brought down by the *Solidarity* trade union in league with the Pope, or the Czech leaders who were defeated by the "Velvet Revolution." Yugoslavia, Poland, and Czechoslovakia had secret police with a well-earned reputation for brutality, yet they quietly surrendered when the moment of truth arrived.

Neither *Solidarity* nor the Czechs were able to mobilize as many people as the Iranians have already brought into the streets of the major cities. This is cause for optimism. It shows that the Iranian opposition is well organized (which is what the mullahs believe; it's why they rounded up the teacher and student leaders in late February 2002, and beat to death two of the teachers), and has both depth and breadth. *Solidarity* had to survive many years of harsh military repression, but most students of contemporary Iran believe that when push comes to shove the Iranian Army will not move against hundreds of thousands of peaceful demonstrators.

But nobody really knows, because nobody can forecast the tempo of change that will lead up to the defining moments in Iran, nor the context in which those moments will occur. Many people confuse themselves by trying to analyze policy options as discrete problems with fixed parameters, but the world is constantly changing and it changes most dramatically when the United States shows up and acts decisively. It's easy to spot these people, because they use a lot of neutral-sounding words, of which their favorite—and their preferred policy—is "stability."

Stability is an unworthy American mission, and a misleading concept to boot. We do not want stability in Iran, Iraq, Syria, Lebanon, and even Saudi Arabia; we want things to change. The real issue is not whether, but how best to destabilize.

Things will change dramatically once we unleash war on the terror masters. In fact, things have already changed considerably. Remember all the gloomy predictions at the war's onset? Remember all those people who told us that Pakistan would erupt in a spasm of Muslim rage if we operated out of Pakistani airfields? That the "Arab street" would go ballistic? All wrong. The Pakistanis were awed, and the Arab street started to honor the traffic signals. No less a pundit than Arthur M. Schlesinger, Jr. gloomily warned us:

> . . . American troops in Afghanistan would
> be even more baffled and beset than they
> were a third of a century ago in Vietnam . . .

... by November freezing weather will arrive, and the Pentagon has no hope of dispatching troops and winning the war in the six weeks before winter comes to Afghanistan. Nor could an invading American army count on serious assistance from the internal anti-Taliban resistance . . .

. . . The last thing we need is a counter-jihad to respond to the jihad invoked against us by the pals of bin Laden . . . [5]

The success of our counter-jihad was part of a rapid transformation of the world that has greatly enhanced our ability to destroy the terror masters. As soon as we were attacked, friendly countries raced to help us, above all by sharing sensitive intelligence about the terror network and its masters. Our intelligence skills have not greatly improved since September 11 (it takes a generation or so), but our information about, and understanding of, terrorism have increased dramatically, thanks to our friends and allies.

Moreover, the very act of getting engaged automatically produces intelligence and understanding that we never could have had otherwise. We have captured great quantities of information in diaries, letters, computerized files and privately published books (like the *Encyclopedia of the Islamic Jihad*). And we have captured thousands of people, some of whom have told us what they know. We are less vulnerable and more powerful than we were in September 2001, and the terrorists are weaker.

Under these circumstances, the greatest strategic mistake we could make is excessive caution. Prudent military planners always want to advance a step at a time, consolidating each victory before moving forward. But the war against the Iranian terror masters is not a question of military conquest; we will not have to send armed forces to capture territory. Our soldiers—in the form of most of the Iranian people— are already on the ground, ready to remove the regime from within.

It was a mistake to dawdle after the destruction of the Taliban and the rout of Al Qaeda in Afghanistan. The delay made our task more difficult, and enabled the hardliners to punish and kill many of their internal enemies.

Iran is not a single, discrete target. It is part of the broader mission, and should be treated like a piece of a broader strategy, just as the terror masters throughout the region are coordinating their plans to fight us on all fronts. At the same time we support the overthrow of the Iranian regime, we will also have to thwart the mullahs' murderous efforts to drive us out of Afghanistan, and their joint enterprise with Syria and Iraq to stage attacks against Israel from their traditional stronghold in Lebanon.

That means we must also destroy the tyrants next door in Iraq and Syria.

Iraq: Revolutionary War Within and Without

Khomeini brought a global vision to power in Iran, while next door in Iraq Saddam Hussein arrived in power in the same year—1979—with a view from his native village, Tikrit. Compared to Khomeini's messianic vision, Saddam's aspirations were parochial; Saddam was not so bold as to proclaim himself the leader of a global Islamic revolution. All he wanted was to rule Iraq, dominate Iran and kill anyone who might threaten his reign. In his first year as tyrant, he decimated his enemies, real and imagined. In his second year he invaded the Islamic Republic.

I have only heard two jokes about Saddam, and they tell us more than most scholarly analyses. It seems that one day, Allah decided that Saddam's time was up, and so he dispatched the Angel of Death to Baghdad to collect him. The Angel of Death flew into one of Saddam's palaces and gave him the bad news. Whereupon Saddam seized the angel by the throat, beat him savagely from his halo to his wings, and threw him in jail, where the angel was tortured for several weeks. Miraculously, the angel escaped and returned to heaven to tell the story to Allah.

Allah listened gravely to the angel's story, and said: "I hope you didn't tell him that I sent you."

The second Saddam joke amplifies the message of the first. Saddam decides it's time to run a routine loyalty check on his cabinet ministers, and calls one of them to him. "Minister," he announces, "I'm going to ask you some questions. Please take your time and carefully consider your answer. It could be important for the rest of your career." The minister agrees, and Saddam asks the first question: "Who is braver in battle, the Iraqis or the Americans?"

"Why, surely the Iraqis," the minister quickly replies.

"And why is that, exactly?"

"Because the Iraqis are not afraid of death, President."

"Very good indeed, Minister. But tell me this: Who is mightier, me or the prophet Mohammed?"

After just the slightest pause, the minister replies, "Why, you of course."

"And why do you believe that?"

"Because the prophet Mohammed is afraid of God, President."

Saddam has killed by any and all means, singly and

en masse. He has used chemical weapons against his own people and against Iranians. He has had his domestic enemies dissolved in vats of acid before his eyes. When his officers defected, he sent them videotapes of the rape and execution of their wives and daughters, and the torture and execution of their sons.

However, in the last days of the Gulf War Saddam had his family smuggled out of the country to a North African redoubt, and his private jet was fueled and ready to get him out, as of the time we decided our mission was accomplished. He's a fierce and brave man (he visited the front during the fighting, something not many national leaders—anywhere—would do), but he's not suicidal.

The regime is modeled on that of his hero, Stalin, complete with the full panoply of repressive secret police and a highly refined cult of personality. He has survived countless attempted coups, and buried countless challengers, for personal power is his primary concern. To that end, he has brought Tikrit— his home district—to Baghdad. Top government positions are routinely given to Tikriti natives, who apparently are the only people Saddam trusts aside from his immediate family (his son Qusay is his currently indicated successor, and, in addition to a substantial oil-smuggling business, runs the press, the country's athletic programs, and an elite guard unit to guarantee the security of the capital). His tyranny is imposed through a traditional tribal system with a veneer of modern management (tribal leaders are simultaneously Ba'ath Party officials).

A man of this sort ("an emotionally insecure megalomaniac with a talent for extricating himself from disasters of his own creation"[6]) uses terrorism to advance his personal interests, not those of the nation or of the faith. His Arab socialist background reinforces these instincts, as they do with the Assads in Syria. Saddam uses terrorists to intimidate other countries near him (he has long funded, trained, and sheltered the Mujahedin-e Jhala, which operates against Iran), to demonstrate he is a major player in the Arab world and in the struggle against Israel (he has supported most of the major terrorist organizations, from Fatah to Abu Nidal, at one time or another), and above all to avenge personal affronts. By far the most important of these is the Gulf War, the loss of which he took personally, as a test of will and strength between himself and Bush the Father. That is why he ordered his intelligence service to kill the elder Bush shortly after the inauguration of Clinton, and he continued to seek revenge thereafter. That he played a role in the World Trade Center bombing of 1993 is highly likely, albeit unproven, and a relationship with bin Laden is as close to certain as you can get in the world of clandestine operations. His intelligence service certainly had contacts with Al Qaeda in Sudan, and Saddam has recently embraced extremist Islam, another element that points to a working relationship with Osama.

> . . . Saddam's regime has lately encouraged the rise, in Iraq's northern safe haven, of Salafism, a puritanical sect tied to Wahhabism that hitherto had been alien to Iraq. It is no surprise, then, that one of these Salafi movements inside Iraq, the Jund al-Islami, turns out to be a front for bin Laden.[7]

The most famous contact between Iraq and Al Qaeda came in Prague, on April 8, 2001, when Mohammed Atta—the key September 11 operative—met with an Iraqi intelligence case officer named al-Ani, working under diplomatic cover at the Iraqi embassy as second secretary and consul. The Czech intelligence service observed the meeting, whose importance can be best appreciated by Atta's travel schedule. He arrived in Prague on April 7 from his residence in Virginia Beach, Florida, and returned home on April 9. Less than two weeks later he opened an account at the Sun Bank in Florida and $100,000 was transferred into that account from an unknown money-changer in the Persian Gulf. That money probably funded at least part of the September 11 operation.

Atta's quick trip parallels an earlier one to the same place. Almost exactly one year before, he flew to Prague from Germany, but he didn't have a proper visa and was blocked at immigration. He returned to Bonn, spent a day getting a visa from the Czech consulate there, and jumped on a bus to Prague the following morning. After less than twenty-four hours in Prague he flew to the United States. So far as I know the Czech watchers didn't catch that meeting.

The meeting between Atta and al-Ani in 2001 did not take place in the security of the Iraqi embassy, but rather on the outskirts of town, which suggests that Atta may not have known his interlocutor's true identity. Al-Ani took a risk by meeting where he could be observed, and an experienced case officer would not do that without a good reason. It seems as if al-Ani believed it was more important to conceal Iraq's role from Atta, than to conceal the fact of the encounter from the Czechs. Al-Ani needed thoroughly plausible deniability for his government in the event Atta were captured and interrogated.

Saddam would certainly have jumped at the opportunity to participate in the September 11 plot, and had good channels to the bin Laden people: His intelligence service was quite familiar with Al Qaeda from their meetings in Sudan, and Iraq, along with Syria and Iran, helped Al Qaeda fighters relocate to Lebanon after their defeat in Afghanistan.

Saddam has always been an integral part of the terror network, working intimately with Syria and Iran in Lebanon. There is considerable evidence that Saddam uses Abu Nidal—who has been based in Baghdad since 1998 after spending several months in Tehran—as the key intermediary in these relationships. Abu Nidal has long been associated with other Palestinian groups such as the Popular Front for the Liberation of Palestine and the Islamic Jihad, both of which have received Iraqi and Iranian support. Moreover, Abu Nidal operatives are based in Palestinian camps, including Ein al-Hilweh in Sidon in southern Lebanon, the Nahr al-Barel camp in Tripoli in northern Lebanon, and other camps in the Bekka Valley, where Hizbollah has long been based. As always in Lebanon, these areas are controlled by Syria.

A recent Iraqi defector who credibly claims to have been a top official in the Mukhabarat—Saddam's security and intelligence service—told *Vanity Fair*'s David Rose of the ongoing relations between Iraq and various terrorist groups.

> The first was the Iranian opposition force
> . . . which during the 1980s maintained at
> least 20,000 fighters inside Iraq, where it
> helped suppress the 1991 Shi'a uprising.
> The second was the Popular Front for the

Liberation of Palestine, which carried out a long string of murders and hijackings . . . However, by the early 90s, the Popular Front's place in the terrorist pantheon was usurped by . . . Hamas, perfecters of suicide bombing. . . . The defector's testimony reveals the true depth of the Iraq-Hamas connection.[8]

The defector painted a detailed picture of the close working relationship. Hamas had its own office in Baghdad, and its own subdepartment within the structure of the Mukhabarat. Hamas killers were trained in Iraq, both at the infamous Salman Pak terrorist camp and another in the northeast. And of course there were weapons, "guns, ammunition both heavy and light, detonators, and explosives. It was Iraq which trained Hamas in how to make bombs."

There are good reasons to believe that Saddam continues to seek ways to take revenge on us, and we know for a certainty that his people are working feverishly to develop several weapons of mass destruction. UN inspectors—who are the first to admit they could not possibly have found everything—documented the production of "9,000 liters of anthrax, 19,000 liters of botulinum toxin, and 2,200 liters of aflatoxin. And that was in addition to huge stocks of mustard, sarin, and VX poison gases."[9]

These frightening numbers are based on the report of UN inspectors, who were expelled from Iraq in 1998. Information from later defectors is even worse: They speak of dozens of secret locations for nuclear weapons research.

Half of Washington was shut down and several innocent people were killed because of a relatively tiny amount of anthrax delivered in postal envelopes. Imagine what could be done with Saddam's enormous quantities, unleashed by a sophisticated delivery system that could put large amounts of anthrax, sarin, or one of his other dread weapons into the ventilation system of major office buildings, or even over a city (we know that some of the September 11 terrorists were in Florida studying the possible use of crop dusters, almost certainly to deliver poison of some sort). Plus, Saddam has a nuclear program, and even if he hasn't built an actual atomic bomb, he very likely has enough radioactive material to build a "dirty" or "radiological" bomb, a conventional explosive surrounded by radioactive material that would be pulverized and scattered over a large area when the bomb goes off.

As John Hackett reminds us,

Saddam invaded his neighbors twice, Iran in 1980 and Kuwait in 1990 . . . and used poison gas extensively during the 8-year war with Iran, killing tens of thousands of young Iranian soldiers, and then sprayed poison gas on a village of dissident Kurds in his own country, killing men, women and children alike.[10]

Iraq would have developed nuclear weapons by now had it not been for the pinpoint Israeli bombing of the Osirak reactor in 1981, an exercise of the right of preventive self-defense that we would do well to emulate. For, as President Bush said in his State of the Union address in 2002, we would be foolish to wait until Saddam actually uses one of these weapons against us before we strike at him. It's likely we won't wait.

U.S. strategic planners of the Iraqi campaign have a fascinating challenge. Saddam is strong enough to cow his domestic enemies, but he cannot survive an American assault. He couldn't survive it a decade ago, when his armies were considerably stronger than they are today. But we do not want to pulverize the country. We want to bring down the regime, just as we did in Afghanistan, and as we will do in Iran. And as in Afghanistan and Iran, we must work with the Iraqi people, our most potent weapon against the tyrannical regime.

We will find them eager to rid themselves of Saddam. It is hard to compare the misery of Iraq with that of Iran, but, if anything, life is more miserable under Saddam than under the mullahs. Accounts of widespread starvation are convincing (although blaming UN sanctions for the famine puts the burden on the wrong party; the Ba'athist elite lives in princely fashion in palaces as large as the centers of major American cities, so there's plenty of money available were the regime willing to spend it on the common good).

Some parts of the Iraqi resistance are known to us, while others will emerge when they see that we are serious. Dissident military officers have repeatedly (and unsuccessfully) risked their lives to gain American support for an armed coup d'etat in Baghdad, but no matter how many are slaughtered by Saddam, more come forward to take up the cause. And they keep coming to us, even though our leaders have repeatedly betrayed them, from the bloody defeat of the northern Kurds and southern Shi'ites at the end of the Gulf War to the terrible fiasco of 1995–1996, when Ahmed Chalabi's Iraqi National Congress was overrun by Saddam's armed forces. These desperate people do not distinguish among American presidents; it does not matter to them whether Clinton or Bush is in charge. But they know they need America's help.

The Iraqi National Congress is out of favor in the State Department and the CIA, as earlier discussed, in large part because Chalabi is not amenable to the kind of strict control our diplomats and spies so often demand. State and CIA do not admit to this. Instead they attempt to discredit the INC by claiming it is ineffective, or that Chalabi and the other leaders are not up to the task. But this is a hard argument to sustain, because Saddam's behavior shows otherwise. He was so concerned about the INC that he sent his army against them, despite stern warnings from Clinton that we would respond violently to any attack.

Furthermore, the INC has shown its potential on the ground, inside Iraq. In late 2001, for example, the INC carried out numerous acts of sabotage, striking at oil refineries, pipelines, and police headquarters. During the Thanksgiving weekend—a nice bit of symbolism—a Shi'ite resistance organization hit one of Saddam's Baghdad palaces with a mortar shell.

Actions of this sort cannot be carried out without considerable popular support, and the INC's many successes disprove the claim that it is hopeless for the United States to support the Iraqi democratic opposition forces. Quite the opposite is true: We are obliged to support them.

As we did in Afghanistan, we need to create a zone of freedom to which Saddam's enemies can repair to find safety and normalcy. We have long proclaimed a "no fly zone" in northern Iraq. We should transform it into a "no trespassing zone," help the

Iraqi National Congress install itself there, and then recognize the INC as the legitimate government of the country. It would immediately become a haven for Saddam's enemies and a staging ground for the democratic revolution. At the same time, we can create a similar zone in the south, where the country's Shi'ite majority is concentrated. Both would come under the protection of our irresistible air power.

These steps should be combined with internal sabotage and an imaginative campaign of psychological destabilization. The CIA wrought havoc on Abu Nidal by playing with his tortured mind, and Saddam's spirit is no more tranquil. Facing outspoken challenges from north and south, coping with daily acts of sabotage against his oil business and his security forces, Saddam may well do what Abu Nidal did: turn his wrath against his own people, and decimate his own protectors.

There are many ways to wage war, and many ways to destroy a tyrant. Especially when you have his oppressed people on your side.

Syria

Future historians of the Middle East will struggle to explain the West's fascination with Syrian tyranny. Henry Kissinger once called Syrian dictator Hafez al-Assad "the most fascinating man in the Middle East," and Warren Christopher made twenty visits to Damascus in a vain quest to bring Assad to the peace table, once sitting in his plane on the tarmac before receiving an undiplomatic snub and flying out without a meeting.

Hafez al-Assad was the sort of dictator Western intellectuals and diplomats find attractive, even though he was not a big personality and never rewarded them for their praise, and even though he was a mass murderer on an historic scale. When members of the Muslim Brotherhood attempted to stage an insurrection against Assad in the early 1980s, he responded by slaughtering between thirty and forty thousand people in the city of Hama, expelling another one hundred thousand, and then bulldozing the center of the city into the sand. And Hafez was as corrupt as the other terror masters, having quietly transferred billions of dollars into European bank accounts. His son and successor, Bashar, has not been openly challenged, so we do not know if he is as ruthless and corrupt as his father, but Bashar referred to the Hama massacre in conversations with American diplomats and congressmen after September 11, brazenly calling it a successful antiterrorist policy.

According to Syrian and other Arab press accounts, Bashar told a visiting American congressional group in January 2002 that "the U.S. can benefit

from the experience of countries that have successfully fought terrorism, primarily Syria."

Subhi Hadidi, a Syrian journalist living in exile in
Paris, angrily commented:

> Logic would dictate that the Syrian regime
> . . . would try as hard as they can to bury
> this accursed memory and refrain from talk-
> ing about it. . . . After all, this was one of the
> bloodiest and most violent incidents of (the
> Assad regime. . . . The Hama massacre . . .
> (is) not an (event) in the fight against ter-
> rorism . . . [11]

Indeed, it was not. It was a bloody repression of all
signs of dissent against Assad's Ba'athist regime
throughout Syria. Had the United States emulated
Assad's methods in Afghanistan, and ruthlessly
purged anyone suspected of sympathy for Osama bin
Laden or the Taliban, it would have been rightly condemned for uncivilized behavior. Yet Assad was "the
most fascinating man in the Middle East."

Some of the American representatives in Damascus were quoted as having been favorably impressed by Bashar al-Assad's advice (although they
later denied it), but none of them mentioned Syria's complicity with international terrorism. Just
two months earlier, following the assassination of Is-

raeli Tourism Minister Rehavam Ze'evi in his hotel room in Jerusalem, credit was claimed in a Damascus press conference by the Popular Front for the Liberation of Palestine. And when British Prime Minister Tony Blair went to Damascus after September 11 to enlist Syrian support in the war against terrorism, Assad angrily replied that he would not lift a finger against the numerous terrorist groups based in his country, because they were fighting to "liberate Palestine."

Not to mention that one of Osama bin Laden's wives had taken refuge in Syria just before September 11, or that terrorists involved in the American embassy bombings in Tanzania and Kenya in 1998 testified at their trial the following year that they had acquired forged passports in Damascus and Latakia.

Syria is as much a part of the terror network as Iran and Iraq, and works hand in glove with Iran to support the deadliest terror organization, Hizbollah. The dreadful terrorist siege against Americans in Lebanon in the 1980s—the bombing of the American embassy and Marine barracks, and the repeated kidnapings and assassinations—needed active support from both Damascus and Tehran, and received it.

Disagreements between the two terror masters invariably revolved around tactical matters, as when, in the late winter of 2002, the Syrians and Iranians debated over who should lead the Lebanon-based terrorist attacks by Hizbollah against Israel. The Iranians supported their long-time operative Imad Mughniyah (recently returned to Lebanon after receiving medical treatment in Tehran), while the Syrians preferred to give operational control to Hizbollah's director-general, Hassan Nasrallah.

Meanwhile, there was no problem in giving support to Al Qaeda, which transferred at least part of its operational base from Afghanistan to Syrian-occupied Lebanon in early 2002.

A senior operative of Osama bin Laden's network, a Yemeni national who has the alias of Salah Hajir, is believed to have arrived in Lebanon two weeks ago and has held meetings in Beirut with leaders of the Hizbollah terrorist group . . .

Donald Rumsfeld, the US Defence Secretary, said: "We know Iran is actively sending terrorists down through Damascus into the Bekka Valley where they train terrorists, then engage in acts against countries in the region and elsewhere."

Although British diplomatic sources said that Hizbollah, a Shi'a Muslim organisation, and Al Qaeda, which is Sunni Muslim, were "unlikely bedfellows," there is substantial evidence of a working alliance between the two groups dating back to the early 1990s. . . . Reports . . . indicated that Hezbollah provided Al Qaeda with explosives and training . . . [12]

Indeed, Syria's support for terrorism is so obvious that you don't even need access to intelligence or diplomatic sources to prove it. All you have to do is read Syrian schoolchildren's textbooks, which present the regime's view that jihad is a "sacred principle to be followed as a personal duty by the students."[13] Syrian school texts, like those throughout the Islamic Middle East, preach jihad as an obligation.

> The believers, the *jihad* warriors, sold their souls to *Allah*. . . . They were killed for the cause of *Allah* and became eternal martyrs. Therefore, they are worthy of *Allah's* Paradise . . . *Allah* brings this news to the courageous *jihad* warriors in order to calm their hearts (so that they may) go fearlessly and enthusiastically to battle. . . . (T)hey are determined to achieve one of two worthy things: victory or martyrdom.[14]

The Syrian regime's support for jihad is not limited to promises of an eternity in Paradise. The families of the fallen warriors have long been the beneficiaries of quite earthly rewards. Western newspaper readers have only recently discovered that the families of Islamic "martyrs" are given substantial amounts of money by Iraq, the Palestinian Authority, and Saudi Arabia, but this practice has been well established in Syria for many years. Indeed the Syrians have created a special place—"The City of the Martyrs' Children"—where the orphans "acquire knowledge and . . . receive compensation for the motherly and fatherly love they have lost."[15] The martyrs' children are supposed to be treated preferentially by all of Syrian society.

Further evidence of the Syrian role in terror is manifest in the regime's actions on neighboring territory. Syria occupies Lebanon—another of the Assads' brutal acts that escapes Western condemnation—and dictates policy on the ground there. Hizbollah is based in Lebanon's Bekka Valley, and could not possibly operate without Syrian approval and support, nor could Iran provide its share of Hizbollah's wealth and weaponry without agreement from Damascus. Moreover, in late 2001 Syria hosted a conference attended by a virtual Who's Who of international terror: the head of Hizbollah, Sheikh Nasrallah; the head of Hamas's political bureau, Khaled Mash'al; the head of Islamic Jihad, Ramadan Abdallah Shalah; the director-general of the Popular Front for the Liberation of Palestine-General Command, Ahmad Jibril, and its Overseas Command Chief, Maher Al-Taher.

To be sure, the Syrians didn't call these men "terrorists"; they were called "leaders of liberation organizations." Whenever the Syrian regime talks about "terrorists," it invariably limits its definition to Israel and the Islamic Brotherhood. Bashar al-Assad has been quite explicit on this point: "We must not allow the charge of terrorism to be slapped on the resistance movements . . . both in Lebanon and in Palestine."[16] And Syria slyly acts to ensure there will be no international campaign against Middle Eastern terrorists, insisting that nothing can be done without the approval of the United Nations General Assembly, and recommending that real control be put in the hands of virulently anti-Semitic and anti-American organizations like the Durban Conference.

Nonetheless, the United States has constantly courted and appeased Syria in the misguided hope that there must be a peaceful pony somewhere in that pile of terrorist and tyrannical manure. Not only did a long line of American secretaries of state beat a dismal path to the door of Hafez and Bashar al-Assad, but even before Ground Zero had ceased to burn, a top CIA official secretly went to Damascus to ask for Syrian assistance in the war against the terror masters.[17] This prompted *The New York Times*'s reporters to remark that "the mere fact of the meeting represents a significant shift in relations between the United States and Syria," but in reality it was simply a continuation of the long-standing American appeasement of Syrian tyranny.

Inviting Syria to join an antiterrorist coalition was as incoherent as the invitation to the Iranian "reformists," and demonstrated once again that our policy makers were either unwilling or incapable of coming to grips with the real nature of the terror network. American leaders persisted in their self-delusion well into 2002. In mid-February, for example, the *Washington Post* reported that the Bush administration "has refrained from confronting Damascus about its illicit imports of Iraqi oil, despite what industry analysts say is a sharp increase in volume."[18] And at his press conference on April 1, 2002, Secretary of Defense Rumsfeld spoke at length about the cooperation among Syria, Iran, and Iraq in support of anti-Israeli terrorism.

Syria is an integral part of the terror network, every bit as important, and every bit as tyrannical, as Iran and Iraq. For many years the Assad family successfully gulled the United States into believing Syria was more reasonable than the others, perhaps because the Assads' Alawite sect does not advocate a violent campaign against Western infidels. But the logic of the war against the terror masters is inescapable. The Syrian regime must join the Iranians and the Iraqis on the heap of failed Middle Eastern lies.

Unlike Iran and Iraq, we must infer the existence of broad-based hatred of the Syrian tyranny; there are none of the public signs of discontent that have surfaced in the other two countries. Yet it would be fanciful to believe that the Syrians are the only people in the Middle East to prefer an oppressive tyranny to a chance to be free. In any event, there will be ample opportunity to find out. Ever since President Bush's "axis of evil" speech, the terror masters in Damascus, Baghdad, and Tehran have been coordinating their plans to defend one another against the expected American attack. Wherever we begin the war, the other two countries will join the fight.

The Saudis

In the months following September 11, we looked at the list of suicide terrorists, saw that the overwhelming majority of them came from Saudi Arabia, and finally realized that we had a big Saudi problem. It had been there all along, but it was hard for us to see it plainly through all that oil and all that money. The September 11 terrorists were not the products of misery or oppression; they were not driven to desperation by lack of financial opportunity or career satisfactions. They were the products of Saudi wealth used on behalf of Saudi religious doctrine to inculcate hatred of us and most everything we stand for. You need only look at Osama to get the picture. He is the son of one of the richest men in the kingdom, and his beliefs came right out of the state-funded radical Islamic schools and mosques.

Saudi Arabia is invariably called a moderate Arab country, but the adjective "moderate" is only accurate if applied to the Saudis' desire for good relations with the West; it is misleading if it is taken to imply that the country is tolerant of dissent, easygoing with regard to the behavior of its citizens or open-minded on the role of religion. On all these questions, the Saudis are extremist Islamists: They are Wahhabis.

Saudi Arabia is as despotic as any Near Eastern country, and it is the only country among its neighbors in which there are no political elections of any sort. Although John F. Kennedy compelled them to let women attend school and university, the Saudis have relegated women to a position of distinct inferiority, and they do not let women drive cars or hold office. The country does not permit the accused to have legal representation in court, which makes life easy for the prosecutors, and press censorship is among the most rigid in the world. And of course there is no religious toleration of any sort; Wahha-bism is the only approved religion. Persons of other religious convictions are not allowed to practice their faith, whether it be another version of Islam or Christianity or Judaism. Corruption is rampant, which is no doubt the main reason they keep the national budget a state secret.

When President Franklin Delano Roosevelt promised American protection to the Saud family in exchange for American access to Arabian oil, he could not imagine that Wahhabi fundamentalism would one day inspire mass murder of Americans. Yet until very recently, the number of American policy makers who knew anything about Saudi-style Islamic radicalism could be counted on the fingers of one mutilated hand. Many self-proclaimed Saudi experts still argue that Wahhabism does not represent a threat against the West, and they deny that the Saudis have set up radical religious schools that advocate jihad and recruit terrorists from among their students.

R. James Woolsey, the former director of Central Intelligence, minces no words on the Saudi role in the terror network: "The Saudi monarchy has had a bargain with the Wahhabis—if you leave us alone, we will help you set up mosques and radicalize young people to your way of thinking. Well, it is a bargain that is not in our interest. That deal, and what it produced, deserve a very large part of the blame for September 11."[19] Professor Vali Nasr puts it even more bluntly: "Saudi Arabia has been the single biggest source of funding for fanatical interpretations of Islam."[20]

But things are even worse than that, because the Saudi "deal" with the Wahhabis is not only tactical; many members of the royal family are true believers and are quite happy to see Wahhabism's poison spread around the world. The intensity of anti-Semitism in the Saudi press is fully the equal of anything that appears in the Iranian, Palestinian, or other Islamic publications. In the Saudi government's daily newspaper, *Al-Riyadh*, for example, a regular columnist provided his readers with this ghastly blood libel in March, 2002:

> I choose to speak about the Jewish holiday of Purim . . . This holiday has some dangerous customs that will, no doubt, horrify you . . .
> During this holiday, the Jew must prepare very special pastries, the filling of which is not only costly and rare . . . the Jewish people must obtain human blood so that their clerics can prepare the holiday pastries . . . the Jews' spilling human blood to prepare pastry for their holidays is a well-

established fact, historically and legally, all
throughout history. This was one of the main
reasons for the persecution and exile . . . [21]

Many members of the Saudi royal family are as
eager as bin Laden to take revenge against infidels
and crusaders, and over the past five to seven years
they have forged closer strategic alliances with
countries like Iran and Syria, in order to wage war
on the West. Foremost among these is Prince Abdullah, the de facto ruler (King Fahd is suffering
from a debilitating disease and has had at least one
major stroke). Abdullah has worked closely with
the Iranian mullahs and Syrian dictator Bashar Assad since coming to power several years ago, and is
himself a devout Wahhabi.

Abdullah's predecessors had generally supported
American foreign policy. The most dramatic example
came during the Cold War, when the Saudis kept
pumping large quantities of oil in order to keep energy prices low, and thereby to prevent the Soviet
Union, the world's second largest oil producer, from
getting too much hard currency via oil sales. While
there were occasional disagreements—most notably
over Israel, which the Saudis loathe as much as any
of the other Arab countries do—they were tamped
down by the overriding common interests. But the
really big conflict went unremarked at the highest

levels of American power, even when the Saudis got very nasty.

In the summer of 2001, Prince Abdullah sent a personal message to President Bush that was unprecedented in the history of U.S.–Saudi relations for its lack of diplomacy. In essence, Abdullah said that either the United States stop Israeli military actions against the Palestinians, or the Saudis would end their strategic alliance with Washington. This from a country whose survival depended on the American strategic umbrella! The White House did not respond immediately, and while President Bush pondered his options, September 11 arrived and put the Saudi question in an entirely different context. Now we began to realize the enormity of our shortsightedness. Just as we had failed to notice the emergence of the terror network itself, American diplomats, intelligence officers, and policy makers had failed to notice that the Saudi royal family was underwriting the terror masters.

By funding religious extremists from Michigan to Mindanao, the Saudis have done their best to destroy democracies, turn back the clock on human rights and deny religious freedom to Islamic and other populations—while the United States guarantees Saudi security. It is *the most preposterous and wrongheaded policy in American history since the defense of slavery.*[22]

But the funding of radical Islamism through the vast worldwide network of religious schools and radical mosques is only the beginning of the Saudi problem. If you read the news carefully, you will see that members of the royal family—those close to Crown Prince Abdullah, who now rules the country—are actively engaged in the operations of the terror network itself.

> In August 2001, King Fahd fired his director of intelligence, Turki al Faisa . . . Turki had anchored the Abdullah faction, and *under his leadership Saudi intelligence had become difficult to distinguish from Al Qaeda . . . Saudi intelligence had served as bin Laden's nexus to the Wahhabi network of charities, foundations, and other funding sources.*[23] (emphasis added)

Public proof of this apparently shocking claim surfaced shortly after September 11. In October 2001, as part of our frantic search for the terrorists, NATO intelligence officers raided the Sarajevo office of the Saudi high commissioner for aid to Bosnia, ostensibly a humanitarian institution to bring aid to suffering

Muslims at the end of the fighting. The Saudis had angrily denied suggestions that the high commissioner's office might also be a front for Al Qaeda, but the raid showed otherwise. NATO officials found:

- computer files with photographs of potential terrorist targets and street maps of Washington, D.C., with government buildings clearly marked

- a computer program with instructions for using crop dusters to spread pesticide

- "before" and "after" pictures of Al Qaeda targets, including the World Trade Center and the U.S.S. *Cole*

- materials for the production of fake credit cards and State Department ID badges.

At the same time, we arrested six Algerians who had been detained by local authorities in Sarajevo.[24] They were eventually among the handful of prime terror suspects transferred to the detention center in Guantanamo Bay, Cuba.

In other words, the Saudi philanthropy was a front for Al Qaeda operations in the Balkans.

Stories like this help explain why the Saudis have been so reluctant to cooperate with American investigators of terrorist activities, even going to such lengths as decapitating potential witnesses. Not only do the Saudi royals doubt our resolve to decisively dismantle the terror network, some of them are part of it themselves, and don't want it dismantled.

Not all of the Saudi royal family was pleased by the growth of Wahhabi power and the growth of the terror network. Some eagerly support it, while others paid "protection money," hoping only to stay out of its sights. But whether or not they enthusiastically funded or encouraged the spread of radical Islam, all of them are complicit. From our standpoint it matters little if, as Paul Michael Wihbey believes, the royal family wants to forestall "an international investigation into the Saudi role in the creation of Al Qaeda," or if they are simply buying security. It all comes to the same thing: The Saudis are funding and assisting the terror network.

They would do better to invest their money in the future of the country. Two decades ago Saudi per capita income was close to our own, but it has dropped a chilling 75 percent over the past twenty years. With oil prices flat or even declining, the kingdom's rulers face a very real prospect of social and political unrest, and not just from the newly impoverished and unemployed, and not even from the fringes of Islamic fundamentalism. Indeed, one of the scions of the ruling elite—Hani Ahmad Zaki Yamani, the thirty-six-year-old son of former oil minister Sheikh Ahmad Zaki Yamani—has written a book[25] in which he criticizes the royal government for mismanagement of the national economy and demands the popular election of the country's "consultative council." Now a mere rubber stamp for the royal family, the council would acquire clearly defined power and responsibility under Yamani's proposal.

Yamani denounces corruption at the highest levels of the kingdom, revealing the poorly kept secret that the Saudis buy expensive advanced weapons systems from the West because of the enormous kickbacks and commissions the weapons sales generate for members of the royal family who invariably act as brokers and consultants.

Finally, Yamani criticizes the presence of American troops and urges the government to establish strategic alliances with the other "moderate" Middle East states (Egypt, Turkey, Morocco, and Pakistan) to guarantee the kingdom's safety.

Yamani's criticisms echo those of the radicals, and suggest the mounting desperation of the elite. They are now trapped between a rock and a scimitar, their power and wealth menaced whichever way they squirm. If they start sharing power with the populace, they will most likely strengthen the most extreme Wahhabi factions; if they retain their dictatorial control over the country, they risk mounting public discontent that may turn violent.

What should the United States do? We clearly cannot tolerate a continuation of the current situation; those hate-preaching schools and mosques must either be closed or fundamentally changed, and as President Bush has repeatedly warned, we will not distinguish between terrorists and regimes that support them. But if the kingdom cuts off all funding of the radical schools and mosques, there will certainly be a violent response from Al Qaeda and, in all likelihood, from the majority of the people.

The Saudi problem highlights the bizarre nature of the Middle East, in which, as Bernard Lewis has repeatedly observed, there are three different kinds of state:

- tyrannical anti-American regimes, in which the people hate the regime, see the United States as the only hope for change, and are therefore pro-American (Iran and Iraq, for example)

- "moderate" Arab regimes, in which the people hold us responsible for the corruption and failure of the regime, and are therefore anti-American (Egypt and Saudi Arabia)

- two states in which both the government and the people are pro-American, because they are the only governments that are elected, and therefore reflect the wishes of the people (Turkey and Israel).

Paradoxically, chances for a decisive, positive change are probably easier to achieve in hostile countries like Iran and Iraq than in Saudi Arabia, because the Iranian and Iraqi peoples see us as the best hope for freedom. They know that Saddam and the mullahs hate us, and have crushed civil society in the name of Islamic anti-Americanism. But the Saudi people view us—fairly enough—as accomplices of the corrupt Saudi regime. They are therefore tempted to join our worst enemies.

Thus, while we can imagine pro-Western and even democratic successors to the tyrannies of the terror masters in Iran, Iraq, and Syria, it is hard to imagine such happening in Saudi Arabia. The Wahhabi poison has penetrated very deeply into the body of the nation, and a "democratic" change might well have the same disastrously antidemocratic result it had in Algeria, where the Islamist extremists won a general election. Many repressive regimes have been swept into power by antidemocratic mass movements, after all.

The Arabists in the U.S. State Department and

the intelligence community, having failed once again to identify a mortal threat to our national security, are reduced to hoping that we will somehow get lucky. They hint that the royal family will jump on the antiterrorist bandwagon once they see the fall of the terror masters elsewhere in the region. If we destroy Al Qaeda, and bring truly moderate, pro-Western governments to power in Syria, Iran, and Iraq, the Saudis, according to these experts, will have much less to fear from dismantling the global Wahabbi network.

It's always better to be lucky than smart, and there is an important element of truth in this hopeful forecast. The massive defeat of the forces of Islamic fundamentalism throughout the Middle East will have a decisive effect on the thinking of Islamic leaders and on the passions of the Islamic masses. The calls for jihad by future Osamas will no longer have their current charismatic appeal, and the awe presently inspired by the terrorists will transfer to our victorious forces.

But we cannot always control our own luck, and unlucky things may happen in Saudi Arabia while we wage war to the north. In the worst-case scenario, the country will be seized by the most radical Wahabbi elements, as a last desperate effort to stave off the impending triumph of the infidel crusaders. In that event we would have to extend the war to the

Arabian peninsula, at the very least to the oil-
producing regions. We would have no other acceptable option, because the West needs Saudi oil, and
we cannot permit ourselves to be blackmailed by a
handful of corrupt petty tyrants.

One doesn't always have the luxury of attractive
options, and prudent planners are obliged to prepare
for unpleasant developments. As we have seen, they
do sometimes come about.

5

FINAL THOUGHTS

Tyranny, like hell, is not easily conquered; yet we have this consolation with us, that the harder the conflict, the more glorious the triumph. By perseverance and fortitude we have the prospect of a glorious issue; by cowardice and submission, the sad choice of a variety of evils.

—THOMAS PAINE

We will undoubtedly win the war against the terror masters, for we excel at destroying tyrannies. The great democratic revolution of the last quarter of the eighteenth century bears an American trademark, and the entire twentieth century shows the awesome power of our revolutionary energies. Again and again we were dragged into war: by the Kaiser into World War I, by Tojo and Hitler into World War II, by Stalin into the Cold War, by Saddam Hussein into the Gulf War, by Osama bin Laden into the war against terrorism. Our enemies always chose the time, place, and circumstances under which the war began. They had all the advantages, yet we defeated them all.

It behooves us to reflect on their motive: Like those who attacked us in the twentieth century, the terror masters started this war because they fear us. Our professional policy makers sometimes forget that America automatically threatens oppressive regimes and would-be tyrannies, but the actual and aspiring tyrants are well aware of our revolutionary power. Behind all the anti-American venom from the secular radicals in Baghdad, the religious fanatics in Tehran, the minority regime in Damascus, and the corrupt kleptomaniacs in the Palestinian Authority is the knowledge that they are hated by their own people. That is why they must use terror to sustain their rule. The terror masters have recently attacked us, but they have always attacked their own citizens. I believe that, given the chance to express themselves freely, the Iraqi, Iranian, Syrian, Lebanese, and Palestinian people would oust their current oppressors. Properly waged, our revolutionary war will give them a chance.

The radical transformation of several Middle Eastern countries from oppressive tyrannies to freer societies is entirely in keeping with American character and the American tradition. Creative destruction is our middle name, both within our own society and abroad. We tear down the old order every day, from business to science, literature, art, architecture, and cinema to politics and the law. Our enemies have always hated this whirlwind of energy and creativity, which menaces their traditions (whatever they may be) and shames them for their inability to keep pace. Seeing America undo traditional societies, they fear us, for they do not wish to be undone. They cannot feel secure so long as we are there, for our very existence—our existence, not our policies—threatens their legitimacy. They must attack us in order to survive, just as we must destroy them to advance our historic mission.

We even do it when it is not explicitly part of our policy, because the rest of the world assumes it is. This was most recently seen in the 1980s, when President Reagan instructed the CIA to organize some Nicaraguans to disrupt the flow of weapons from Nicaragua to the communist guerrillas in El Salvador. The operation envisaged at most a few hundred people. But once American officials went into the field to recruit, thousands of Nicaraguans, assuming this was the beginning of the end for the Sandinista regime in Nicaragua, raced to sign up. A few years later, the Sandinistas were voted out of office. A few years from now, the terror masters will no longer be in power.

It will be more difficult for us to win the peace. Our track record on this score is mixed. We did it well after World War II, and we did it badly after the Cold War and the Gulf War.

After World War II, recognizing that years of Nazi and fascist indoctrination had paralyzed the ability of the German, Italian, and Japanese people to think and act like free human beings, we insisted on the total elimination of all former Nazis and fascists from positions of prestige and authority, and on the rejection of fascist and Nazi doctrines from public discourse and the educational systems. Paradoxically, we advanced the cause of freedom by violently undemocratic means, imposing the rules of a free society on nations that had fought against the very idea of freedom, teaching them the rules of democratic politics, and remaining engaged in their affairs until democracy had clearly been established. This was a great success, as proven by the flourishing democratic societies in contemporary Germany, Italy, and Japan.

Unfortunately we did nothing of the sort at the end of the Cold War. Indeed, some of our leaders acted as if they were embarrassed at the defeat of the Soviet Empire (remember the unfortunate "chicken Kiev" speech by Bush the Elder, when he asked the oppressed people of the Ukraine to "abandon their wild hopes for independence"? Or his later appeal to Yeltsin to support Gorbachev's scheme to hold the Empire together?). Our leaders boasted of their consideration for the tender psyches of the former Soviet leaders, and we delicately avoided any celebration of their defeat.

It was a mistake. We should have publicly identified all the officials in the Soviet Empire who had actively supported the communist tyranny, and we should have insisted that the archives of the Kremlin be open to the public, so that the peoples of the fallen Empire could discover their real history, and could distinguish among those who were enthusiastic supporters of the dictatorship and those who were compelled to compromise with the regime. And we should have helped the newly freed peoples learn the rules of democratic society, by getting directly engaged in creating new political institutions and writing new textbooks and encyclopedias. Some of this was done, but precious little. Had we been more active, and had we shown that we recognized the glory of our victory and the rightness of our cause, we would probably not now see so many former communists in positions of power in the former Soviet bloc.

The same mistake was made at the end of the Gulf War. We should not have left the Middle East battlefield without bringing down the regime of Saddam Hussein. It is perhaps understandable in psychological terms, but it is nonetheless strategically misguided for people like General Brent Scowcroft and former President George H. W. Bush to insist to this day that they were right to leave Saddam in power. Had we seen the war through to its proper and logical conclusion, and installed a representative government in Baghdad, we would probably not be facing the challenge of the terror masters today. We certainly would not have to worry about Iraqi weapons of mass destruction being unleashed on us or other Western countries.

We must hope that our leaders will not repeat these mistakes, and that, once the tyrants in Iran, Iraq, Syria, and Saudi Arabia have been brought down, we will remain engaged, just as we must remain active in Afghanistan. This time we must ensure that we win the peace, not just the war. We have to ensure the fulfillment of the democratic revolution.

Some experts are skeptical that proper democrats can be found inside tyrannical countries like Iran, Syria, and Iraq. It is worth reminding ourselves that brilliant men—like George F. Kennan, author of the "containment doctrine" that shaped our Cold War strategy—doubted there were any real democrats in Nazi Germany after Hitler's defeat. These pernicious doubts led Kennan then, and lead some of our policy makers now, to conclude that democracy cannot succeed in such circumstances, and we would do better to reach an accommodation with people in power on the grounds that only the current leaders have the necessary managerial and political skills to maintain stability.

Kennan was wrong—Germany's thriving democracy proves that—and the skeptical diplomats and analysts of the present moment are equally wrong. There are undoubtedly plenty of good democrats throughout the Middle East, and they will openly embrace our common cause as soon as we demonstrate its success. Success can be accomplished in one of two ways: We can forcibly destroy the tyranny, as we did to Germany, Italy, and Japan in World War II, or the regime can lose its nerve and crumble from within, as occurred in the Soviet Empire under Gorbachev.

Throughout modern history democrats have studied and organized quietly within tyrannical regimes. In recent years, examples have ranged from Poland's *Solidarity* during the communist era to the popular resistance to Ferdinand Marcos in the Philippines and the Yugoslavs' uprising against Slobodan Milosevic. Just as many Polish democrats involved in the "underground university" traveled to the West to discuss how best to achieve a transition to democracy, today many Iranian and Arab democrats are in touch with counterparts in the United States, Europe, and even Israel, laying the groundwork for future Middle Eastern democracies. Like the Poles under Soviet domination, the Middle Eastern democrats depend on the discretion of their Western friends for their security, and we will only see the results of their efforts once the tyrants have been overthrown.

A local example shows how easy it is to underestimate how oppressed people understand their condition, and how wrong it is for us to assume that there are no democrats just because we do not see them. Some years ago I worked with an ABC News television crew that produced a documentary program on the tiny island of Grenada one year after its liberation by American armed forces. Several members of the ABC team had been in Grenada during the previous Marxist dictatorship of Maurice Bishop, and had always found Bishop to be highly popular. Now they heard very different stories. Most everyone complained about the harshness of the oppression and the misery of daily life. One day, interviewing a citizen with whom he had spoken in years past, an ABC producer asked, "But why didn't you tell me this before? I was here, we knew each other, you could have told me."

"Oh no," the man replied, obviously surprised at the naiveté of the question, "it would have been too dangerous to tell you. I could not do it."

If we had a CIA worthy of the name we would know more about freedom-seeking people in countries like Syria, Iran, and Iraq, and among the Palestinians who groan under Arafat's corrupt tyranny and know they can do better. A first-class intelligence service would know the people and support them. Alas, we do not know them, and we have not supported them. As we destroy the regimes and the networks of the terror masters, we will come to know the democrats, and we will find them fighting alongside us.

The war against the terror masters is a special case of a broader problem, one that has been faced by other republics at moments of crisis. How can we reconcile our democratic values with the necessity of imposing our will on our enemies? This problem was elegantly engaged by the late Luigi Barzini in an essay about Julius Caesar:

> The venerable virtues which had made the simple and sturdy Latin farmers invincible and allowed them to conquer vast possessions and immense wealth were clearly inadequate to govern those very possessions and to administer their new wealth. They had to transform themselves and reform the State. Yet their very greatness was rooted in their obsolete virtues . . . without them they would have become decadent, effete, corrupt, and impotent. This . . . is the problem of many successful republics, whose simple virtues make them strong enough . . . to conquer other people and assume imperial responsibilities. How can men, who are dedicated to liberty and the defense of their own independence, efficiently dominate subject peoples, without damning their own soul?[1]

The American answer is that we do not want to "efficiently dominate subject peoples," we want to free them. The United States is not going to wage war against Iran, Iraq, and Syria in order to turn them into American colonies. As Oriana Fallaci wrote, America "is born of a spiritual necessity . . . and of the most sublime human idea: the idea of . . . liberty married to the idea of equality." We believe that our ideas are more powerful than those of the terror masters, and that, once liberated, the peoples of the Middle East will embrace our ideas and join with us.

Finally, as we wage this war, we must constantly remind ourselves of five basic rules of successful political and military leadership, as defined half a millenium ago by Machiavelli. They are as true today as they were during the Renaissance, at the beginning of the modern era:

1. Man is more inclined to do evil than to do good.

Good people are rare, and are constantly threatened by the evil-minded. Peace is not the normal condition of mankind, and moments of peace are invariably the result of war.

Since we want peace, we must win the war. Since our enemies are inclined to do evil, we must win decisively and then impose virtue, until the people learn the rules of civil society.

2. The only important thing is winning.

Machiavelli tells us that if we win, everyone will judge our methods to have been appropriate. If we lose, they will despise us.

3. If we have to do unpleasant things, it is best to do them all at once.

Strike decisively, get it over with quickly. The diplomats will always say that we can achieve our goals with a little bit of nastiness and a whole lot of talking, but they are wrong.

4. It is better to be feared than loved.

We can lead by the force of high moral example. It has been done. But it's risky, because people are fickle, and they will abandon us at the first sign of failure. Fear is much more reliable and lasts longer. Once we show that we are capable of defeating our enemies, our power will be far greater.

5. Luck can wreck the finest plans.

Machiavelli played cards whenever he had the chance, and he knew that a bad run can ruin the finest player. Machiavelli ruefully admitted that the best one can hope for is to have good luck about half the time. But that should be enough for us. We're a lot stronger than the terror masters.

6

LOOKING FORWARD

In March 2002 it already seemed to me that we had waited too long to take the battle to the Terror Masters in Baghdad, Tehran, Damascus, and Riadh, and we had still not acted in June. This delay gave the terror states an opportunity to buy further time by convincing the Bush administration that it had to make an all-out effort to "solve" the Israeli/Palestinian matter before moving to the "next stage" in the war against terrorism. This argument was advanced by several

American friends and allies, but most importantly and effectively by the Saudis. They were by then greatly alarmed by the growing body of evidence in the American and West European press that showed the intimate connections between the royal family and the terrorist organizations, as well as the Saudis' ongoing funding of the global network of radical Wahhabi schools and mosques in which young Muslims were taught to hate Western infidels.

As I had written last winter, the Saudis and Europeans had it backward. The Palestinian question was logically a post-war issue, not a precondition for waging war. Some of the most brilliant statesmen in the world had labored for more than half a century to craft a durable peace between Israel and the Palestinians. All had failed. Why should anyone believe that there was any real chance to solve it in the spring of 2002? It's more reasonable to believe that a fundamental change in the region is required to advance peace, and that those calling for new rounds of negotiations were using it as a pretext to stall our war effort.

Moreover, anti-Israel terrorism had long ceased to be a purely Palestinian phenomenon, if, indeed, it had ever been. This book shows that there has been an intimate relationship between Palestinian and Iranian terrorists for thirty years, and, as before, the terrorist assaults against Israel in the first half of 2002 were supported by the Iranian regime, with strong backing from Syria, Iraq, and Saudi Arabia. To summarize the earlier argument, Iran runs the most important organizations, Syria provides the facilities for training and the safe havens, Iraq chips in intelligence and money, and the Saudis "reward" the families of the suicide terrorists.

Further evidence of the true nature of the terror network emerged in early June, during celebrations in Tehran. The Ayatollah Ruhollah Khomeini, the founder of the Iranian Islamic Republic and the central figure in the creation of modern Islamic terrorism, died in 1989 on the thirteenth day of Khordad, the third month of the Iranian calendar. Thirteen being a famously unlucky number, the Iranians celebrate Khomeini's death on the lucky fourteenth, which fell on the fourth of June. In honor of the great man, 167 top leaders of twenty-five terrorist organizations gathered in Tehran for a two-day conference on "Support for the Intifada." They included all the usual suspects, including seven representatives from Al Qaeda, all the radical Palestinian groups, Iran's own Hizbollah, and officials from twenty-five friendly countries.

The terror summit came at a time of considerable internal agitation and intense Iranian support for terrorist activities against the United States, Great Britain, and Israel. As usual, the country's internal problems catalyzed its external violence. Just two weeks earlier the Ayatollah Ebrahim Amini, the deputy leader of the Council of Experts—perhaps the most powerful institution in the Islamic Republic—publicly warned that the country was on the verge of insurrection. Amini gravely observed that "the people are unhappy with the injustice . . . of the . . . regime," and he warned his colleagues that they could not expect to retain power by the use of repressive force. Still darker warnings came from Hojatolislam Niazi, who heads the legal council of the Armed Forces. Niazi reported the existence of extensive plots in the holy city of Qom to overthrow the regime and warned "we are fully aware of their secret meetings."

The Iranian peoples' mounting desperation and disgust with the regime was driving them to take more and more overt action against the mullahs. A week earlier a group of armed young people in the city of Lamerd in Fars Province attacked the Revolutionary Guards' headquarters, badly damaging the building. Army troops had to be called in to put down the uprising, which, as you will know from the earlier text, was only the latest of many.

Despite Ayatollah Amini's admonition against the use of repressive force, the regime moved in the opposite direction. Interior Minister Lari ominously announced that the "crisis center"—a particularly nasty group of special forces and trained assassins—has again started to act. A few days before the June Fourth conference the Revolutionary Guards attacked buses carrying students on tour to the historical sites in Gomen, arresting seventy-three young men and women, killing two of them. Mohammad Khordadian, a noted folk dancer who lives in Los Angeles, returned to Iran six weeks earlier to attend his mother's funeral, only to be arrested at the Mehrabad airport and locked away, accused of "corrupting youth." And one day after the conference, the so-called Nationalist-Religious Group published photographs of the torture of Mr. Vahid Sadeqi, one of their activists. He was seized outside his home in Shiraz and dragged off to a safe house where, according to his account to Radio Free Europe–Radio Liberty, acid was thrown on his arms, the hair on his chest was set on fire, "truth serum" was injected in his veins, and the names of three historic Iranian leaders were carved into his back with knives and burning cigarettes. Photographs of Sadeqi were distributed in Tehran, to the consternation of the regime.

This sort of information is not supposed to circulate in the Islamic Republic, whose leaders have been at pains to shut down any publication that reports the regime's evildoing. As I write, virtually every Iranian newspaper worthy of the name has been shut down, six others are facing judicial action, several books have been confiscated and banned, and judicial action has been undertaken against several members of the hapless Parliament. On the other hand, two of the assassins of Mr. Dariush Foruhar, the distinguished leader of the secular Iranian People's Party, had their life sentences commuted to ten years' imprisonment after the regime claimed that Foruhar's family forgave the murderers. This bit of patent nonsense was quickly denied by his daughter Parastoo, who lives in Germany.

Even fun came under assault. Roadblocks manned by the Basij—the regime's version of the fascist storm troopers—routinely stopped cars playing forbidden western music, and if unmarried women were found in the company of men, they were arrested and charged with moral corruption. Thirty people were arrested in Tehran a few days before the conference, and eighty more were picked up in Fuman, all accused of "illegal and immoral behavior." Single women can be subjected to humiliating virginity tests, and if they flunk the exam they are given the option of marrying or being flogged.

The regime also cracked down on simple expressions of opinion, most notably those in favor of normal, open relations with the United States. The Iranian people are probably the most enthusiastically pro-American in the Islamic world, and would love to see an active American presence in their country.

The regime, at least publicly, constantly attacks the United States, and has banned any discussion of normalization of relations from all media, and even in school classrooms. When two journalists challenged the decree, they were quickly issued subpoenas.

These are only a few examples of the widespread repression of the Iranian people who, as President Bush remarked in his State of the Union address, have shown a great desire to be free of their self-appointed regime. The mullahs are trying hard to deprive the Iranian people of all hope, and to that end they have intensified their terror campaign against the United States and its allies. Their aim is to drive Americans out of Afghanistan by the same means Khomeini adopted in Lebanon in the 1980s: by killing and kidnapping Americans, and eventually demonstrating that the United States does not have the staying power to win. The conference in Tehran showed the regime's determination and also the considerable support they enjoy from the other terror masters.

Early in 2002 the Iranian regime provided chemical weapons to the Palestinian terrorists, and in honor of Khomeini's anniversary they contributed 314 (third month, fourteenth day) of their best missiles to Iranian-sponsored terrorists in Afghanistan, under the control of their henchman, Hekmatiar. Of these, 200 were ground-to-ground rockets of their

own design, along with 64 surface-to-air and 50 an-
titank missiles from their friends in Russia, China,
and North Korea. All were fully assembled and were
scheduled for deployment against American and British forces in Afghanistan. Moreover, the American
government received credible information in early
June that Iran was racing full speed ahead on a nuclear weapons program, an ominous development in
light of earlier statements by Rafsanjani and Khamene'i that nuclear war in the Middle East might
well destroy Israel, but not Iran, because Iran was too
big and could well absorb millions of dead in a nuclear exchange, and the little-noted remark at a press
conference in May by Russian Deputy Chief of Staff
General Yuri Baluyevsky, asserting that Iran already
possessed nuclear weapons.

Iran's intention to assault our soldiers was not a
secret; hardly a day passed without a leader of the
regime pronouncing it. While some of the details of
Iranian terrorist activity in Afghanistan and elsewhere
in the region are not known, we know enough to
justify serious action against the regime in the name
of self-defense, and the legitimate desires of the Iranian people have been acknowledged and praised by
the president himself, by his national security adviser,
and by the secretary of defense. Yet, as of mid-June
we still had no Iran strategy. There was no coordi-
nated public policy, such as radio and television

broadcasting in Farsi, a sustained condemnation of the mullahcracy by our own leaders, and material assistance for those leading the freedom movement inside Iran. It is hard to imagine that the Iranian people required enormous support to rid themselves of their meddlesome priests, and, unlike the challenge we faced in Iraq, one could readily imagine a successful regime change in Tehran without dropping a single American bomb or firing a single American bullet.

We have done it before. When the Soviet Empire was brought down, much credit was justly given to Western radio stations that broadcast to the citizens of the Empire in their native languages. Although the Kremlin strove desperately to prevent the people of the Empire from learning what was really going on, both inside Soviet borders and in the world at large, the people were able to listen to the truth from the BBC, Voice of America, Radio Liberty, Radio Deutsche Welle, Kol Yisrael, Vatican radio, and others.

In like manner, the terror masters in Tehran strive to prevent their people from learning the truth, by jamming foreign broadcasts, tearing down satellite dishes that can receive Farsi-language shows from Europe or Los Angeles, by shutting down any newspaper that dares criticize them, and by arresting, torturing, and murdering those brave enough to openly oppose them. The American government today should be doing to the Iranian regime what we did to the Communist regime in the 1980's: pro-claiming its evil nature to the world at large, and above all to its own oppressed citizens, and assuring them that we stand with them in their struggle for freedom. And we should support the organizations inside Iran that are prepared to challenge the tyrants, just as we helped Solidarity in Poland.

Such a policy would be entirely in keeping with our national tradition of fighting tyranny, and, if suc-cessful, would have a decisive effect on Muslims everywhere. If the regime in Iran is brought down with our help, it will demonstrate to the Islamic world that radical Islamist regimes, whether the Sun-nis in Afghanistan or the Shi'ites in Iran, ruin their countries, alienate their people, and are ultimately defeated and humiliated by the United States.

This is precisely the message we want to send, for at the end of the day we must show the Muslims that they have been led astray by the terror masters, that they should look within themselves for the source of their centuries-long failure, and that the best hope for them lies in cooperation with the civilized world and in greater freedom for all their people. We want them to realize that Turkey is a more desirable model than Iran, Iraq, Syria, Saudi Arabia, or Afghanistan under the Taliban, and we want them to look to us as a source of support and friendship.

As usual in such matters, the longer we wait the

more difficult our task will be, and the higher the price we will have to pay. The terror masters have made contingency plans, and it is unlikely that we still have the luxury of dealing with Iran, Iraq, and Syria one by one. They probably come bundled, and wherever we start, we should expect a vigorous response from all three countries. If we had moved quickly after the fall of the Taliban and the rout of Al Qaeda, we could probably have limited our actions to just one of the three; now it is more difficult and our mission will have to be more ambitious.

But the reverse is also true: Wherever the revolutionary war against the tyrants begins, it will quickly spread to the others. Our strategy should therefore be regional, not limited to a single target, and the best way to do that is to deploy our strategic assets quickly: Recognize the Iraqi opposition as the legitimate government of the country, prepare to defend them against any military attack from Saddam, coordinate our public policy to support the Iraqi, Iranian, and Syrian people, and get material support to them.

As this book went to press, there were many hints that the Bush administration was in fact moving in this direction. The clearest signs were public: the statement by the president on the tenth of June that the time was not ripe for a new round of peace talks between Israel and the Palestinians, and his speech to West Point graduates a week earlier in which he spoke of the need for pre-emptive strikes against terrorists. There was also private evidence along the same lines, especially from administration "hawks," who, without providing details, expressed confidence that the political winds were now shifting in their favor.

Meanwhile, the president announced a dramatic reform among the bureaucracies dealing with homeland security, one piece of which was badly needed: the creation of the domestic equivalent of the CIA's Counterterrorism Center. By bringing top analysts to a single place, and giving them all the information collected by the myriad intelligence and law enforcement agencies dealing with terrorism, Bush dramatically increased our chances to spot terrorist activity before an actual assault takes place.

The rest of the reorganization is harder to evaluate, and in any case no bureaucratic move can deal with the central problem that afflicts our intelligence services, because their main weakness does not derive from poor structure, but from poor culture. For more than twenty-five years they've been hammered by the media and Congress. They've been hamstrung by guidelines so restrictive that as of September 10 the FBI was not even permitted to clip newspaper articles for their files unless they had reason to believe the people and organizations described in the articles were engaged in criminal activity, or preparing to commit criminal acts. And the CIA was not permitted to work with people who might have had "human rights issues" in their past. That leaves us with a generation of intelligence practitioners who have never been aggressive (the aggressive ones have mostly left government service), and who have learned all the wrong lessons: Don't take chances, don't push your superiors to bring forward information that demands action.

Read Bob Baer's memoir, or Reuel Gerecht's various essays, and you will find that the CIA gradually eliminated from its ranks any gung-ho officers who really wanted to get to the heart of the terror network. And that was only logical, because for at least twenty-five years the top people weren't going to act, and so they didn't want to hear the gory details about the terrorists. Such information would make them uncomfortable, and they didn't want it.

Over time, these rules became habits, and the intelligence community now has a set of instincts that prevent them from getting, analyzing, and interpreting hard intelligence on terrorism. How else can you explain the fact that as of September 10 we had not a single human agent in Iran, Iraq, or Syria? Or that, even months afterward, the director of central intelligence was proclaiming to Congress that there could not be active cooperation between the PLO and Iran, because Sunnis and Shi'ites didn't work together, when in fact they had been working together for thirty years?

September 11 wasn't primarily the result of poor bureaucratic organization, or poor communication between the various agencies. All these existed, to be sure, but they were not the fundamental cause of the debacle, and fixing them won't transform the government's ability to get the terrorists, or bring down the regimes that sponsor them. To do that well requires political will and brave leaders.

That is why I believe the president has to rid himself of those officials who failed to lead their agencies effectively, along with those who lack the political will to wage war against the terror masters. The top people in the intelligence community need to be replaced, and those military leaders who tell the president that it can't be done, or they just aren't ready, or we need to do something else first, should be replaced as well, along with the people in the national security community who insisted that we must solve the Arab-Israeli question before the war can resume and the top people in agencies like the FAA, the INS, and so forth.

Bureaucratic fixes may help something, but they won't solve our current problem. We need war leaders, not compulsive negotiators or management consultants.

Machiavelli, as usual, has the last word. If you win, he tells us, everyone will judge the means you used to have been appropriate. The important thing, indeed the only thing, is to win the war. There will be time enough to worry about bureaucratic wiring diagrams.

7

THE OVERTHROW OF
SADDAM HUSSEIN

Operation Iraqi Freedom was an important battle in the war against the terror masters, but only that. One terror master down, at least two—Syria and Iran—to go. Nonetheless it was a watershed in recent history, and in at least one respect it was a world-historical event: with Prime Minister Aznar's brave support of the Coalition, Spain once again became a major player in international affairs for the first time since the defeat of the Armada by Queen Elizabeth's Royal Navy in 1588. It would have been better to support the democratic revolution in Iran and Iraq before sending our armies against Saddam Hussein, but we were in any event engaged in a regional conflict and—our strong desire to the contrary notwithstanding—would have to deal with all the terror masters, regardless of where the first step was taken.

The battle for Iraq had many positive results. Contrary to much of the conventional wisdom, it strengthened and expanded our alliances with several important countries, from Spain, Italy, Denmark, and the Netherlands to the new democracies of Central and Eastern Europe. It also delivered a potent blow to the terror network. Not least, despite early setbacks and continued confusion—all of which was normal and predictable—the people of the Middle East could see that the Iraqis had in fact been liberated from a terrible dictatorship, and were entitled to dream of a day when they would be free as well.

Nonetheless, errors were made, including some very serious ones. Several of the strategic mistakes I had feared were in fact committed months before the fighting started. The first was the long delay following the liberation of Afghanistan. I had found the delay excessive when this book first went to press in June 2002, and, incredibly, it dragged on for nine more months. This incurred a considerable cost to the two main leaders of the "coalition of the willing": President Bush and Prime Minister Blair.

By all accounts, Blair insisted that any military campaign in Iraq required first one, and then a second approval from the United Nations Security Council, even though there was sufficient legal justification already in place. The Gulf War had never been officially terminated. The fighting had indeed ended, and a cease-fire had been agreed on, but there was no peace treaty. Saddam had, on his own account, violated several conditions of the cease-fire, from the production of chemical and biological weapons (confirmed by the Iraqi government itself as late as 1998) to the manufacture of missiles with ranges longer than those permitted. On this basis alone, the United States and Great Britain could have gone back to the Security Council, announced that Iraq was in material breach of her obligations to the UN, and resumed Desert Storm.

For whatever reasons whether because the Downing Street lawyers felt resumption of military activity required a UN endorsement, or because Blair believed there was a political imperative for a ratifying vote from the Security Council—the British insisted that we go back to the UN.

This had three unfortunate effects: the time required to assemble the necessary votes permitted the opponents of military action (France, Germany, and Russia in the front ranks) to organize an effective opposition (something that could not have been done if the efforts to remove Saddam's Ba'athist dictatorship had followed hard on the fall of the Taliban), it gave the terror masters more time to organize their collective strategy, and it forced a drastic redefinition of the mission itself.

The International Opposition

No one on this side of the Atlantic expected that Jacques Chirac—the first foreign leader to fly to America after September 11 to declare the solidarity of his country and his people with the United States— would do everything in his power to stymie our efforts to bring down Saddam Hussein. We had assumed that France was a loyal ally. Even though the French had often nibbled around the edges of American national security, and had often waited until the very last minute to join with us in such military campaigns as Desert Storm, we reasoned that France could not fail to join Operation Iraqi Freedom, because they had too much at stake. France had huge oil interests in Iraq, and they had to know that once Iraq was liberated, any country that had failed to join in the effort would go to the back of the line of countries wanting to do business with the new Iraq. Instead, Chirac not only exerted prodigious efforts to prevent us from winning final UN approval for Operation Iraqi Freedom, lobbying third-world Security Council members from

South America to Africa to vote against us, he continued his campaign even after the final die had been cast and we were moving our forces into the region. Chirac was particularly effective in Turkey, which is a largely untold story.

The Turks had recently elected an Islamic government, for the first time since Ataturk's revolution at the end of the first World War. That government was not eager for trouble with the United States, and it supported a motion in parliament to permit Coalition forces to use bases in Turkey to stage an invasion of northern Iraq. Had the government imposed party discipline and demanded a unanimous vote, the measure would have passed, but the Turkish leaders—as almost all American experts and diplomats expected—thought that the opposition parties would, in any event, support the motion. But the opposition voted unanimously to reject the motion, and they did so largely as a result of French and German blackmail.

The Turks have long been eager to enter the European Union, but the French have always blocked it. Chirac (with German Chancellor Schröder's endorsement) told the Turkish opposition parties that if the measure passed parliament, Turkey could forget about entry into the EU so long as Chirac decided French foreign policy. Hence the striking unanimous vote, contrary to the opposition parties' longstanding close and friendly relations with the United States, and, not least, contrary to Turkey's economic interests. The United States had promised the Turks about $15 billion in assistance and investment in return for their support of Operation Iraqi Freedom, and the offer was canceled once the votes were counted.

The blackmail of Turkey was a serious setback to the Coalition's military mission. It shut down the northern front for many days, probably prolonged the war for a week or so, and thereby cost some number of Coalition and Iraqi lives. For President Bush, actions of this sort were not those of an ally, but of an enemy. It is hard to imagine that Franco-American relations can be very good so long as Jacques Chirac is in the Elysée, and George W. Bush is in the White House.

The question of French motives is fascinating. Some think that Chirac actually believed he could head off the Coalition attack, and save Saddam, by using the United Nations. Others think that Chirac, and with him Schröder and Putin, sought to use the UN in an effort to limit American power. The French military cannot effectively cooperate with American armed forces (in Kosovo, for example, French Air Force missions had to be accompanied by American fighter planes to protect the outmoded French aircraft), its one aircraft carrier is in dry dock more often than not, and French communications are not up to the most recent NATO standards. France can only play a major role in the United Nations, the European Union, and Francophone Africa. Thus, the French are irresistibly drawn to those fora in its quest for grandeur.

But these explanations are unconvincing, because they do not account for the central fact: France deliberately and openly acted like an enemy of the United States. This suggests a strategic decision rather than an existential tantrum. It is possible that Chirac decided that American power had to be limited, and in order to do that France needed a potent ally, capable and willing to attack us head-on. That ally was radical Islam. France would use its influence in Europe and the UN to shield the terror masters from American power, and in return the terror masters would serve French interests by humiliating the United States whenever possible. Finally, France would reap enormous financial benefits from Saddam, the mullahs, and the Saudis.

We do not know the full story, but time will tell.

The Strategy of the Terror Masters

The most surprising thing about the battle for Iraq is that some of our leaders seemed surprised to discover that both Iran and Syria were sending thousands of terrorists into Iraq to attack Coalition forces. There was no reason for surprise. There was plenty of information to that effect, many months before the start of Operation Iraqi Freedom, and I flatly predicted it in the first edition of *The War Against the Terror Masters*. Moreover, both Bashar Assad in Damascus and Ali Khamene'i and his fanatical allies in Tehran had publicly announced that America would sink into a Vietnam-like quagmire in Iraq, and Assad explicitly spoke of repeating the Lebanon scenario (when Hizbollah terrorist attacks, hostage seizures, and mass demonstrations convinced President Reagan to withdraw American military forces in the mid-1980s). The Syrians were caught red-handed, opening their border with Iraq to terrorists moving east and weapons and Ba'athist hierarchs fleeing west. As usual, the Iranians took greater pains to cover their tracks, but even so, there was abundant information about their operations. In the middle of the war, for example, many Iraqi leaders—reportedly more than a hundred in all—made it by bus across the border to Iran, were escorted onto a commercial aircraft, and were flown to a safe haven in Sudan.

The true audacity of Tehran lay in their political moves, which were driven by the mortal fear of the mullahs that they were next in line. The Iranians infiltrated more than a hundred highly trained Arab mullahs from Qom and other Iranian religious centers into Iraq, especially to Najaf and Karbala, the most holy cities of the Shi'ite faith. There they poisoned the minds of the (largely uneducated) Iraqi mobs with a simple slogan, repeated five times a day in the mosques: "America did it for the Jews and for the oil." They also distributed cash to the Iraqis.

Just as they did against the Shah, the Iranian Shi'ite leaders intended to build a mass following, leading to an insurrection against us. Anyone looking carefully at the banners carried by the Shi'ite demonstrators in the days after the fall of Baghdad could see that they were remarkably clean and well produced, with slogans in both Arabic (for the Iraqis) and English (for Western media). That was the Iranian regime at work, one of the most brilliant and patient intelligence organizations in the region.[1] The slogans chanted by the mobs in Baghdad were Iranian slogans, calls for an Islamic state.[2]

The Iranians combined this political strategy with terrorist acts and assassinations, as in the case of the very charismatic Ayatollah Khoi in Najaf in March. He was a real threat to them, because of his personality and his solid pro-Western views. So they killed him immediately after the fighting stopped, and they planned to kill others of his ilk, along with as many Coalition soldiers as they could murder. Thousands of Iranian-backed terrorists have been sent to Iraq, from Hizbollah killers to the remnants of Al Qaeda, from Islamic Jihadists to top Iranian Revolutionary Guards fighters and officers. Even the head of the

Iranian Intelligence Service, Ali Panahi, went to Karbala to organize the anti-American uprisings, and was headed for Baghdad thereafter.

We did not take suitable precautions against these threats. The Associated Press reported on April 19, 2003, that "there wasn't a single U.S. military checkpoint Friday along the length of the 50-mile road from the eastern city of Kut to the (Iranian) border . . . Iranian border guards roamed freely to the Iraqi side, acting as if they were in charge of the area and quickly asking reporters to leave."

We could not defeat these operations with military power without imposing a level of repression against civilians that would rebound against us; we had to use the Iranians' own methods to defeat them.

Our best strategy consisted of two programs, one defensive and one offensive. The first was to support pro-Western, pro-democracy mullahs in Najaf and Karbala. Most Iraqi people do not like the Iranians, but only their own religious leaders can credibly expose the Iranian operation. They will not fully believe our radio or television broadcasts, or speeches from American generals, but they will listen to their own religious leaders. Similarly, it is next to impossible for us to identify all the Iranian-backed terrorists, but the Iraqi Shi'ites can do it, once they are convinced that their real salvation lies with us. That is why the battle for the minds of the Iraqi Shi'ites was so crucial. By early June, we were working more effectively with Shi'ite religious leaders.

The second program was to support the anti-regime forces inside Iran. That insane regime was very frightened, both of us and of their own people. The ayatollahs knew that the Iranian people long to be free, and the regime intensified its repression during the runup to the war. But the State Department had no stomach for a showdown with the mullahs, and the CIA was not convinced that the Iranian democratic opposition was sufficiently strong, organized, or effectively led to warrant confidence in a quick political victory. Thus, even though everyone agreed that Iran was the most dangerous and most fanatical of the terrorist regimes, that the country was in open ferment, and that Iran's nuclear weapons program was very far advanced (by early summer, the CIA concluded that the mullahs were likely to have the bomb by year's end), there was no Iran policy as of the beginning of June 2003. Even when our man in Baghdad, Ambassador L. Paul Bremer, sent cable after cable demanding more information and firmer action against Iranian-sponsored actions within Iraq, the administration was unable to define an Iran policy.

A thoughtful Turkish general once remarked that the trouble with allying with the United States is that "you never know when the Americans are going to turn around and stab themselves in the back." We won a dazzling military battle, but victory in the war against terrorism was still very much in peril. We were up against a desperate enemy with great skill and cunning, and the cynical ruthlessness that comes from an ancient civilization that has survived countless invaders and occupiers over many millennia.

The Redefinition of the Mission

American policy called for "regime change" in Iraq long before September 11. It was voted by Congress in 1998, embraced by Clinton, and confirmed by the Bush Administration. In actual practice, the Clinton Administration had sought to overthrow Saddam even before it became official policy, as the embarrassing story of the CIA's many failed efforts to organize a coup d'état in Baghdad shows so clearly.

The problem with getting UN approval for the removal of Saddam Hussein was that there were no procedural precedents for it. If we wanted UN approval for the liberation of Iraq, the only available "hook" was the many Security Council votes asserting that Saddam had to dismantle his weapons programs. That is why we opted to link the war against Saddam to the several UN resolutions calling for him to effectively disarm. While this greatly increased our chances to win a vote in the Security Council, it narrowed the debate. Instead of calling attention to Saddam's long-standing support for terrorism, his despoiling of the Iraqi people, and his violations of the cease-fire agreement, we focused all our diplomatic energies on insisting that Saddam disarm. The combination of a suddenly altered strategy and the attendant delay changed the entire focus of both the national and international debate, greatly weakening our case.

Most people understood that the United States was entitled to respond to an attack on our soil, and would have accepted an anti-terror campaign that moved relatively quickly from Afghanistan to Iraq. But once we waited, and then made Saddam's weapons the central theme—early in the fall of 2002, more than a year after September 11!—further delay and an increasingly incoherent policy debate automatically followed.

Moreover, the focus on Saddam's weapons temporarily placed control over the start of the Iraq campaign in the hands of people who were viscerally opposed to any further military action: the United Nations Security Council (where the French and the Russians both had vetoes) and the inspectors, who for the most part were the same people who had been systematically deceived by Saddam in the 1990s. Neither Kofi Annan nor Hans Blix was eager to assume responsibility for unleashing the Coalition armies on Iraq, and their strategy was the same as Saddam's: drag out the process, keep talking, and hope that the Americans would eventually back off.

Finally, our long paralysis was the result of a fundamental misconception of the war itself, which is what I had most feared. The proper goal of the war against the terror masters is fundamentally political: the overthrow of the tyrannical regimes that support the terror network. Yet, from the very beginning, the Bush Administration failed to use the most effective political weapons at its disposal. The violent internal battle over the legitimacy and efficacy of the Iraqi National Congress between the State Department and the CIA, on the one hand, and the Pentagon on the other, frustrated any chance of creating a viable political counterforce to Saddam's regime.

Since the war against the terror masters is fundamentally political, for the most part it should be waged with political weapons. The battle for Iraq was poorly conceived, because it was almost exclusively a military campaign; the political ingredients were few and largely ineffective. The bulk of the political action was carried out by the CIA, which approached the problem in the usual way: by offering money ($200 million was distributed in Basra alone) in exchange for facilitating the overthrow of the Ba'athist regime. This was not successful (the liberation of Basra was carried out by British military forces).

A successful political campaign required an alliance with Iraqis. Simply marching into the country and handing out $100 bills was not good enough. But the administration had disarmed itself, and went into Iraq without an effective political weapon.

The roots of the failure to design and conduct an effective political strategy against Saddam Hussein went back to the early 1990s. Neither Clinton nor Bush forced an end to the debate over the Iraqi National Congress, the key to a successful democratic revolution.

The United States had been at war with Saddam Hussein since Gulf War I, and for most of that period key government agencies in Washington—notably the Department of State and the CIA—fought the INC, even though it was demonstrably the most effective, most representative, and most democratic anti-Saddam Iraqi organization. It would seem elementary common sense to use an organization that can speak to the people as one Iraqi to another, give them guidance that is untarnished by the accents of Americans who betrayed the Iraqis in the past, and credibly explain the democratic goals of the Coalition forces. The INC was no mere exile group; it had fought ground battles against Saddam's armed might and caused the dictator such anxiety that he sent a tank column against it in the mid-nineties, violating the cease-fire agreement in the face of Clinton's warnings.

Instead of enlisting this powerful political/military weapon, both the State Department and the CIA continued to treat the INC and its leader, Ahmed Chalabi, as pariahs, even after the battle for Iraq began. While CIA personnel ran all over southern Iraq with millions of dollars in cash trying to buy the co-operation of the locals, the INC, simmering in its northern redoubt, was deliberately cut off from any way of effectively communicating with the population at large, of taking the lead in the liberation of parts of the country (in one terrible blunder, the CIA actually drove the INC out of a city after it had been liberated by Chalabi's forces), or of talking to the U.S. government without its conversations being intercepted by Saddam. Throughout most of the fighting, Chalabi himself had one outdated secure phone with which he could reach only one top American official: NSC Iraq coordinator Zalmay Khalizhad, a man not noted as a bureaucratic heavyweight. No CIA officer deemed it useful to work with the INC until quite late in the war, despite the organization's impressive track record of intelligence collection and understanding of internal Iraqi events.

The State Department and the CIA were so determined that the INC not play a significant role in the liberation of Iraq that they resorted to bureaucratic skullduggery to silence and paralyze it. In the late nineties the INC launched a television station—

Liberty TV—out of a small flat in London, relayed to Iraq by satellite. There was overwhelming Congressional support for expanded INC broadcasting, as well as for more aggressive political action and information gathering inside the country, but the Department of State and the CIA opposed the ambitious programs. This was a Catch-22, for how could the INC have an effective broadcasting program if they weren't permitted to go inside Iraq to discover the truth? More time was lost, until even the State Department's Inspector General found the INC information program squeaky clean. But even this was not enough to remove the road block.

Despite a Congressional appropriation of more than $90 million to support the INC, the State Department continually found ways to slow the flow of funds to a trickle, and managed to shut down Liberty TV in May 2002. When members of Congress screamed, the Department of State repeatedly promised to provide the money, but found tricky ways to prevent the station from going back on the air—such as providing funds for current expenses but forbidding the payment of past debts to the satellite provider.

Under pressure from Congress, the Defense Department, and the White House, the State Department sent some desperately needed money to the INC office in London two weeks after the fighting began, and told questioners that it was up to the INC itself to move the money from London to Iraq. But that was yet another dodge, for the London office was run by a character named Sharif Ali, who was imposed on Chalabi by the State Department and the CIA, and who had no stomach for the conditions under which the other leaders are now living in northern Iraq. Ali did not find a way to get the money into the theater.

The failed Basra uprising would undoubtedly have benefited from ongoing radio broadcasts from the INC, and might have inspired similar insurrections elsewhere in Iraq, but the American government deliberately, tenaciously, and systematically deprived the Coalition of this essential political weapon. We prepared the battlefield militarily, but not politically, and both we and the Iraqi people paid a price for it.

The distrust of the INC, and the misguided belief that Iraqi support could be purchased rather than won, reflect a cultural failure within the diplomatic and intelligence communities of the United States. There is a congenital reluctance to work *with* foreign groups and individuals. The Agency and the State Department want them to work *for* us, so that we can make all the key decisions, and we can control all the main actors. Ahmed Chalabi would not accept a role as an American puppet, especially because he believed that he knew more about Iraq than the American diplomats and intelligence officers who tried to tell him what to do.

The cultural failure goes even deeper, alas. The attitudes evinced by the CIA and the State Department are profoundly anti-democratic. I argue earlier in this book that many of our government's Middle East experts are subtly racist, because they act as if Muslims and/or Arabs are not capable of self-government. They believe that all such countries will be governed by a thug, and the central policy issue is, which thug? Thus, the insistence that we control groups like the INC. Thus, the endless quest for a successful coup d'état instead of supporting freedom fighters in Iraq. Thus, the two "decapitation" strikes, designed to eliminate the Saddam Hussein family in a single stroke—high-tech coup attempts that seemingly failed, as had the previous seven or eight.

CIA defenders whisper that the first precision bomb attack—the one allegedly aimed at Saddam's secret bunker—did not actually strike the bunker itself, because government lawyers would not permit it (it would have killed too many innocents). Instead, it hit nearby. This reminds me of the old joke of the drunk groping around on his hands and knees under a streetlight. When a passerby asks him what he's doing, the drunk replies, "I dropped some change down the block." "So why are you looking *here*?" The drunk replies impatiently, "Because here I can see what I'm doing."

And even CIA stalwarts have told me that the second decapitation strike—the one on the Baghdad

restaurant—was probably based on unreliable intelligence. Common sense suggested that the intelligence was highly unlikely right then and there: on a
day when allied forces had entered Baghdad, why in
the world would Saddam decide that it was the perfect moment to take his crew out to a neighborhood
restaurant?

The self-imposed failure to have reliable Iraqi allies on the ground before the onset of the fighting
was huge. It delayed the victory, it deprived us of the
kind of enthusiastic welcome from the Iraqi people
we had anticipated, it made the political reconstruc-
tion of the country far more difficult, and it undoubtedly raised the casualty toll. We will continue to pay
the costs of this failure for quite a while.

Operation Iraqi Freedom

There were two early war stories—widely ignored by
what used to be called "the mainstream media"—that
warranted close attention. The first was a report from
Lebanon on the second day of the war, in which the
infamous terrorist group, the Palestine Liberation
Front, announced that one of its men, a certain Mr.
al Baz, had been killed by American missiles in the
first "decapitation" strike.

The story was very important for two reasons.

First, it gave us a bit of revenge. The PLF was commanded by a monster named Abu Abbas, who masterminded the hijacking of the Italian cruise ship *Achille Lauro* in the mid-1980s. During that operation, the terrorists segregated the Americans from the others, and the Jews from the others, and then picked an American Jewish paraplegic, Leon Klinghoffer, and pushed him overboard in his wheelchair. We captured Abu Abbas in Iraq at the end of the fighting, giving us still greater satisfaction.

Second, the story shows the intimacy between Saddam and the terrorists: al Baz was either at a meeting of regime hierarchs, or in the immediate vicinity, where only trusted persons would be permitted.

The second story was in an Associated Press report on the Arab League summit in Cairo shortly after the fighting started: "Libya's secretary for African affairs, Ali al-Treiki, led the Libyan delegation and warned the ministers that, 'If Iraq is to fall, many Arab countries will fall as well.' "

This dynamite story explained the desperation with which so many Arab broadcasters and journalists tried to portray the war as an American debacle and a graphic demonstration of the heroism of Arab fighters. They all feared the contagion of freedom—al-Treiki was not referring to the possibility of a Coalition occupation of the entire Middle East. He was simply stating what the tyrannical terror masters all

believed, namely that if there were a successful liberation of Iraq, and a transition to a civilized and
democratic government, all the tyrants in the region
would be threatened.

There's yet another reason for the importance of
this story: Ali al-Treiki and his Arab League cohorts
knew something that an entire generation of State
Department and CIA Arabists did not know: that Arabs do desire freedom.

This is not the place to discuss the remarkable performance of American fighting men and women, except to say that it greatly impressed the world at
large. The "shock and awe" of our advanced military
technology had been discounted by the millions of
people who had heard all about it long before we
went into action. But few anticipated the remarkable
energy, courage, diversity, and intelligence of our
troops.

The impact on the Islamic world is likely to have
been considerable, especially if we successfully transform Iraq into a relatively secure, democratic country. The terrorist leaders had long proclaimed that
Americans would never be manly enough to fight
hand-to-hand, that we were unwilling to take risks
on the ground, and that we would not tolerate significant casualties. Saddam himself likely believed a
lot of this, and was obviously taken by surprise at the
audacity, speed, and violence of the war plan. Finally,

the makeup of the American forces conveyed a visual image that impressed the Iraqis, and, through them, the entire region. The multiethnic, multicultural American armed forces—a Chinese-American Marine officer named Chin tied the Stars and Stripes on the statue of Saddam in Baghdad, and then returned to attach the Iraqi flag—was something the Islamic world was not prepared for.

This impact would have been even greater had we gone into battle side by side with large numbers of Iraqis. A week into the war, Ahmed Chalabi quietly suggested that it might be easier to induce the surrender of Iraqi soldiers if they were approached by Iraqi opposition leaders rather than by American military officers. He mentioned in passing that his soldiers had been ordered to await the arrival of Allied liaison officers. Such officers should have been with the INC and other resistance forces from the get-go.

The most disappointing part of Operation Iraqi Freedom was the performance of the CIA. That was only to be expected; you can't resurrect a failed organization in a year and a half. As I write, there is a firestorm of criticism over the failure to uncover Saddam's weapons of mass destruction, and the Director of the CIA, George Tenet, has gone on the record to defend the Agency's performance. Unfortunately, it will be a difficult task, for not one of the sites that the CIA had identified as a probable location of

WMDs panned out. Indeed, the Agency's information was so bad that the government had to send a new group of investigators to Iraq in the hunt for Saddam's weapons.

I have little doubt that Saddam had such weapons, but, as I wrote before the war started, he smuggled substantial quantities of them to Iran and Syria, and he arranged for his own escape to Damascus. I was also told that the best places to look for hidden stores of WMDs was beneath Shi'ite holy places, such as the Shrine of Ali in Najaf, and deep underneath oil pumping stations, especially those associated with the illegal pipeline to Syria. As before (for example, the secret tunnel network in Iran described earlier), these underground facilities were said to have been constructed with help from China and North Korea. I do not know if these sites were ever carefully examined, or if the CIA took seriously reports of this nature.

Whatever we eventually find—and obviously if we find nothing at all—there can be no doubt that the CIA had misplaced confidence in the accuracy of its own information on the locations of WMDs, as it had been wrong in predicting it could buy an insurrection in Najaf and the defection of top Iraqi military officers early in the military campaign, and had bought into dubious intelligence about Saddam's movements within Baghdad. Combined with its previous history of opposing the most promising ally in the campaign against Saddam, it confirms the low state of our intelligence.

Bad intelligence invariably leads to bad policy, and this held true in Iraq.

All of which once again raises the question of accountability. I have argued ever since 9/11 that one of this administration's greatest shortcomings is the reluctance to hold people accountable for their failures. No one was asked to resign after September 11, and no one has been asked to resign after Operation Iraqi Freedom. By comparison, the Marines immediately replaced a field commander just because he moved too slowly. That is an excellent example for the administration, which should consider replacing those who counseled delay during those long months between the liberation of Afghanistan and Operation Iraqi Freedom, along with those who produced poor intelligence before and during the fighting. Nothing is better for the morale of a large organization than concrete demonstrations that the top leaders are watching, that failure will be instantly punished and valor instantly rewarded. Thus far, the only people fired by this president were the members of the first economic team.

That said, it is hard to believe the accusations of the many antiwar and anti-Bush people who accused the administration of deliberately falsifying intelligence in order to be able to accuse Saddam of hiding his WMDs, when in reality the CIA and MI6 knew all along that there were none. If the critics wanted to point to examples of distorted intelligence, there were some readily available. But they didn't comment on them, because they would have shown the opposite of what they desired. For example, intelligence was used by Colin Powell to make a case against Iraq's support for the terror network that actually showed the involvement of other terror masters. But the broader picture was narrowed to focus on Saddam. The clearest case is that of Abu Musab Al-Zarqawi.

Abu Musab Al-Zarqawi's name and photograph became front-page items in both the United States and Europe when Secretary of State Colin Powell, in his speech to the UN Security Council, identified Al-Zarqawi as an Al Qaeda terrorist working out of Baghdad.

European antiterrorist experts in Germany and France, who have arrested many of Al-Zarqawi's followers in their countries, vigorously denied any knowledge of a link with Iraq (to have done otherwise would have undermined their governments' antiwar position), but their many denials concealed facts they were reluctant to proclaim: the Al-Zarqawi story was not limited to Iraq, and the terror network of which he was a crucial link extended from many Middle Eastern countries throughout Europe, and into the United States.

No doubt there was a connection between Al-Zarqawi and Iraq—Director of Central Intelligence George Tenet was not sitting right behind Powell to endorse a fantasy—but that is only a small part of the story. Al-Zarqawi's footprints led unerringly to Iran, from where he directed murderous operations in Jordan and Western Europe. And one didn't need anonymous sources to prove it: it was on the record in Germany and Italy, at a minimum. One large body of evidence was available from the Federal Court of Justice in Karlsruhe, Germany, in connection with the trial of one Shadi Abdallah.

Abdallah is a twenty-seven-year-old Jordanian who went to Pakistan in 1999 for religious studies. En route he stopped in Mecca, where he was recruited into the terrorist universe by Osama bin Laden's son-in-law, Abdallah Al-Halabi. Following Al-Halabi's instructions, he traveled to Pakistan and was taken to Kandahar, Afghanistan, where he went to a military training camp. After nearly three weeks of training he was injured, and transferred to a hospital and subsequently to bin Laden's apartment complex, where he was befriended by Osama himself. In short order he became one of bin Laden's bodyguards, and then was introduced to Abu Musab Al-Zarqawi in Kabul. Al-Zarqawi explained to him that the goal of his organization—Al Tawhid—was the overthrow of the Jordanian monarchy, and he invited Abdallah to go to Jordan to participate in the organization. Abdallah declined, and Al-Zarqawi sent him to Germany in mid-2001 (Abdallah had lived there previously) to organize terror attacks against Jews and Americans. Arrested by German authorities late last year, Abdallah turned state's evidence against his comrades, and his testimony is quite recent; his latest interrogation dates to September 2002.

According to Shadi Abdallah's testimony (much of it confirmed by intercepts and other human sources), Abu Musab Al-Zarqawi was based in Iran, and the head of Al-Zarqawi's German operation— known variously as Ashraf, or Noor, or Noureddine, or Hamada—came directly from Iran at the beginning of 2002. Iranian connections abound: terrorists routinely entered Europe with false passports obtained in Iran; information often came via telephone calls from Iran; important orders came via courier from Iran, as did money and forged documents, and on at least three known occasions the head of Al-Zarqawi's German operation traveled to Iran to meet with Al-Zarqawi in order to get instructions.

The German information, of which this was only a minuscule part, showed the Iranian regime up to its neck in terrorist operations all over Europe, but the German authorities did not seem to have uncovered the link to Iraq. That information had probably not been shared with them, at least prior to Powell's speech.

A similar pattern emerged from Italy, where antiterrorist operations rounded up significant numbers of Arab terrorists. Top terrorist leaders were recorded in many conversations with their superiors in Iran (and the Italian documents thoughtfully provide the telephone numbers). Perhaps the most significant of the terrorists arrested in Italy was Abdelkader Mahmoud Es Sayed, an Egyptian active in Islamic Jihad, led by Ayman al-Zawahiri, the chief deputy to Osama bin Laden.

Es Sayed worked in Milan at a mosque, which he turned into "the most important European station for the activities of the Egyptian terrorist organizations Al Jamaa Al Islamiya and [Islamic] Jihad." His contacts ranged from people in the United States to the man he addressed on the telephone as "mawlana," "our master," Rifa'ai Ahmad Taha Mousa, the "Emir" of Jamaa Islamiya. The telephone call was between Italy and Iran, where the emir was located. An additional detail is worthy of note: the two discussed the movements of couriers between Iran and Italy, some carrying written letters, others carrying verbal messages from Iran to the operatives in Europe. Es Sayed's home was found to contain detailed travel instructions to Afghanistan, invariably crossing Iranian territory, along with the interesting instruction that if a traveler were asked his native country, he should say he was Iraqi, whatever the nationality of his passport.

Es Sayed was even on good terms with Defense

Minister Mustafa Tlass of Syria, who gave him telephone numbers for Hamas and Islamic Jihad, telling Es Sayed "talk to them . . . call them . . . they know you." And Es Sayed was also in close contact with Saudis who were using business "cover" to obtain advanced technology for military and paramilitary operations.

European security services routinely share this sort of information—this too is abundantly documented in the transcripts and analyses of the German and Italian governments—so they know that the various organizations work intimately with one another, and find support from several of the terror masters. Their outspoken skepticism about an Iraqi connection was therefore disingenuous (just as Powell's unstated implication that Al-Zarkawi's main base of operations was Baghdad); at a minimum they should have said "we don't have the Iraqi information, but we do know quite a bit about Iranian and Syrian connections." They did not say this because they know that this information would compel them to act on an even broader scale.

The same goes for the Bush Administration. It is understandable that Secretary Powell focused very tightly on Iraq in his speech; that is the issue of the day. But the war against terrorism is only just beginning, and the terrorist armies arrayed against us are working together, thanks to the support of many regimes.

8

WHAT NEXT?

At the end of Gulf War I, the Iraqi occupiers had
been routed from Kuwait, the road to Baghdad was
wide open, the northern Kurds and southern Shi'ites
were ready to overthrow Saddam's murderous dictatorship, Saddam had sent his family abroad and was
preparing his own escape, and the entire Arab world
awaited the imposition of an American imperium.
Had they been in the Americans' position, they
would have reshaped the region in accordance with

their own interests, and they expected us to do the same.

Above all, they expected us to continue to Baghdad, to bring down Saddam's regime, and to install a government of our own liking. Contrary to legend, many of the Arab governments wanted us to do just that. Indeed, the Saudis themselves encouraged us to see the war through to a total victory that would have given us enormous leverage over future events, and not only in Iraq. For example, there was a possibility of eliminating the radical PLO (which had fully supported Saddam) from its dominant position, bringing a new generation of Palestinians to the bargaining table, and creating a Palestinian State that would live in real peace with Israel.

Instead, we stopped on a dime, settled for an inconclusive and poorly designed cease-fire, brought our troops home, and abandoned the Kurds and Shi'ites to Saddam's butchers.

I called it "Desert Shame" and it laid the groundwork for the disastrous decade that followed. Having won an impressive military victory, we sabotaged our own interests during the period of "peace" that followed. Having pressured the Saudis to cut off their traditional funding of the PLO, we soon implored them to resume it. The message spread throughout the region. Arafat regained his strength, those Palestinians who wanted real peace were enfeebled, and terrorism was revived. Having granted Saddam a stay of execution, we stood by as he reestablished his tyranny, crushed the scattered remnants of the opposition, resumed support of the terror network, and reinstituted his weapons programs. We soon betrayed the Iraqi opposition forces in the north, sending an unmistakable message to the entire region: the United States was not prepared to assert its values and its will in the Middle East. This laid the groundwork for the cycle that followed: more confident enemies, including the members of the terror network, assault after assault against Americans and American allies (foremost of which is Israel), and then September 11.

Desert Shame was a pyrrhic triumph of legalistic technicality and diplomatic guile over the relentless pursuit of our national goals. The legalism was real enough, albeit only to those who wished to be prevented from achieving total victory: we had assembled a coalition to expel Iraqi forces from Kuwait, and we felt obliged to stop at the borders of Iraq, even though many of our coalition partners encouraged us to continue.

The wishful thinking was of a sort that continued to undermine our mission ever since: we convinced ourselves that there was no need to risk American lives or treasure, since the locals would do the job by themselves. This dovetailed neatly with the legalistic and diplomatic self-delusion, leading us to act as if the combination of public diplomacy (expressing our hope that the Kurds and Shi'ites would overthrow Saddam) and the political consequences of our military victory would produce the desired result without forcing us to dirty our hands in further actions, or tie us down in a feared Iraqi quagmire.

The situation in Iraq after the battle was eerily reminiscent of Desert Shame, even though many of the self-imposed restraints did not exist. Just as it was a mistake to conceive of Desert Shame as simply a battle to drive Iraqi troops out of Kuwait, our mission in Iraq should not have been merely "regime change" in Baghdad. We should have considered it one battle in the war against the terror masters in Iran, Iraq, Syria, and Saudi Arabia. It should have been seen as just one piece of the overall mission, not an end in itself. It was folly to believe—as so many had to confess they did believe—that we could deal with Iraq alone, and then work out a strategy for the others.

As in 1991, many of our leaders expected that the spectacle of our victory in Iraq would have an inevitable ripple effect throughout the region, and that the Iranian people (for starters) would fulfill their oft-demonstrated dream of overthrowing the mullahs in favor of a democratic system.

But life is not often like that. If we want a free Iran and a free Syria—and we must, if we really want to win the war against terror—we will have to fight for it. Not militarily, in these cases, but certainly politically. Even as we prepared to invade Iraq, the Iranian and Syrian dictators increased their bloody repression, desperately trying to stave off their own day of reckoning. And of course the Iranians sent contradictory messages, cursing us as agents of the devil, only to turn around and sing sweet songs of "better relations" even as they pursued a nuclear program that may be on the verge of fulfillment.

Those who were surprised at the vigor of the Syrian/Iranian operations against us inside Iraq failed to realize that we were perforce involved in a regional war, whatever our desires might be. It was undoubtedly more manageable to focus our attention on Iraq, with its many vexing problems, than to move ahead against the other terror masters. But it was extremely shortsighted to believe that we could "manage" Iraq so long as the mullahs in Tehran and Bashar Assad in Damascus remained in power.

The shortsightedness of the secretary of state and his top people was of a piece with the self-deceiving culture that had led to 9/11 in the first place. Iran was obviously the keystone of the terrorist structure— the State Department's own list of terror-sponsoring countries had shown that for many years. Anyone who listened to the daily tirades from Supreme Leader Khamene'i or strongman Hashemi Rafsanjani would be in no doubt about the intense hatred of the Iranian regime for the United States—the so-called "great Satan." President Bush repeatedly stressed that the war against the terror masters was a struggle to spread liberty throughout the tyrannical countries of the Middle East, and Iran was clearly one of the most tyrannical.

There was therefore no possible compromise with such a regime, which incarnated the Axis of Evil. Yet Deputy Secretary of State Richard Armitage proclaimed Iran "a democracy," and secret talks were held throughout the winter and spring of 2003—talks that were exploited by the Iranians to discourage their domestic opponents—and only suspended when it was discovered that the Al Qaeda terrorists who commanded the May 2003 suicide bombings in Riyadh, Saudia Arabia, were based in Iran. And even then, Powell vowed that the talks would be resumed, and that there would be no change in Iran policy. It was a curious bit of braggadocio, because there was still no Iran policy at that time.

Just as we had convinced ourselves that others would do the necessary dirty work in getting rid of Saddam Hussein, we indulged in the same illusion regarding the mullahs.

As in 1991, failing to pursue our maximum interests risked defeat and humiliation. If the Iranians succeeded in creating a rabid Islamic Republic in Iraq, we would in fact be even worse off than we were with Saddam, and the same vicious cycle would start up again, at a higher level of violence. The rulers of Middle East tyrannies would be enormously strengthened, and the various leaders of the terror network, from bin Laden to Mughniyah, from Al-Zarkawi to al-Zawahiri, would gain new followers and resume their jihad with new fervor.

It was therefore disconcerting and discouraging to see the National Security Council's top man on Iraq, Zalmay Khalizhad, sneaking off to Geneva for the secret meetings with representatives of the Iranian regime, and to see Secretary of State Powell enthusiastically traveling to Damascus. If the State Department was so desperate to talk to Assad, then they should have made him cross the Atlantic and crawl to Washington to beg for survival. Assad took the occasion to lie to the secretary of state; he promised to close terrorist camps and offices, but continued not to do so. Worse still, Powell's trip to Damascus sent a dangerous message to the entire region. By going there instead of summoning Assad (as befit a superpower), we showed weakness. And all serious people in the Middle East remember that, on the verge of a glorious victory in 1991, the same man called upon this president's father to stop short, turn around, and leave the forces of freedom in the Middle East at the mercy of the tyrants.

The Iranian Threat

Although there is still no Iran policy, it is only a matter of time before we are forced to challenge the clerical regime in Tehran. The mullahs will not leave us in peace in Iraq, and they will continue to use their "foreign legion" against us wherever they can, as they did in Saudi Arabia in May 2003. Although the discoveries of Iranian connections in Iraq and Saudi Arabia were greeted with surprise by both our intelligence community and the Department of State, many other important intelligence finds had demonstrated the same link, and had shown that the working relationship in fact went back to the mid-1990s, as I had written.

The first of these was a training manual for terrorists produced by the Iranian Intelligence Ministry, and used to train Al Qaeda in Sudan. The manual—described by a top British terrorist expert as "the mother of all training manuals"—was discovered by British military forces in a Muslim sector of Bosnia in February 1996. It was held for analysis by the British Government until 2002, when it was first made available to private experts. As of this date, it has not been translated into English, although that is presently in the works.

The manual was discovered in the course of a military strike against a terrorist training camp in Pogorelica, in the course of which four Iranian "diplomats" and eight Bosnian Muslims were arrested. The manual was used by the Bosnian Government in the prosecution of three former Bosnian Muslim intelligence officials in 2002. The claim that the manual had been used earlier in the Sudan to train bin Laden's people comes from a person familiar with the results of the interrogations that led to the Bosnian prosecution.

Unlike the "terrorist encyclopedia" described earlier, there is no ambiguity about the provenance of the training manual. It comes from the MOIS, the Iranian Intelligence Ministry. And while the "encyclopedia" is a potpourri of information, some good and some next-to-useless, the manual is a professional product, altogether worthy of one of the world's most skilled intelligence organizations. It contains detailed instructions on everything from clandestine communication, the construction of secure terrorist cells—including recruitment and morale building—simultaneous paramilitary attacks, the use of explosives, kidnapping, countersurveillance methods, and extended sections on jihad against the West.

The manual helps us understand the evolution of Al Qaeda to a world-class terrorist organization. It wasn't entrepreneurialism that got them there; it was training by one of the world's chief sponsors of terrorism.

The manual also expands the number of cases of

Sunni-Shi'ite cooperation against their common Western enemies, and again shows the silliness of the widespread view that the two branches of Islam are in perpetual conflict.

Finally, the manual shows that the Iran–Al Qaeda partnership continued after bin Laden left Sudan for Afghanistan, and probably constituted one of the leit- motifs of the history of contemporary terrorism.

The other document that suggested ongoing co- operation between the Iranian regime and Al Qaeda was even more explosive, although its credibility is open to question. In late May 2003, I was told by reliable sources in Europe that they would soon have a copy of an internal regime document that would prove close working relations with Al Qaeda. At the end of the month, I received a fax of the document, and a color photograph of it was posted on a Farsi- language Web site.

The evidence consists of a letter, dated early May 2001, from the head of the intelligence group in Su- preme Leader Khamene'i's office, Ali Akbar Nategh Nouri, to a Mr. Pourghanad, the head of "Operational Division Number 43," which appears to be a special forces unit of the Revolutionary Guards, operating under Khamene'i's direct command. Nouri repeat- edly makes it clear that he is speaking in Khamene'i's name, and tells Pourghanad that the top goal of the Iranian regime is to fight the United States and Israel, and to "inflict wounds to the economies and to harm other organs of these two allied enemies of Islam, and to endanger their system of justice and their sense of security is a necessity as a way for settling political accounts with them."

To that end, Pourghanad is instructed to work closely with the leaders of Al Qaeda and Hizbollah to join forces to achieve the single objective of attacking the United States and Israel. Nouri warns that the special group must be very careful not to leave any "footprints," as this could produce "negative effects." And Pourghanad is told to limit his communications and his coordination activities to just two people: Imad Mughniyah, the operational chieftain of Hizbollah, and Ayman al-Zawahiri, the operational commander of Al Qaeda. He stresses that Pourghanad must do as he is told: "Have no doubts as to cooperating with Al Qaeda, and keep up the present connections."

If true, the letter is a bombshell, for it proves intimate working relations between the top operational commander of Al Qaeda and the office of the Iranian supreme leader, just four months before September 11. If confirmed, it would abruptly end any hope of a modus vivendi between the United States and Iran, and most likely with the European Union as well. It would galvanize American policy makers, above all those who would feel that we had been duped by the Iranians for a year and a half.

I know of more than half a dozen Farsi-speaking

experts who have examined the letter, and all found it credible. It contains several signatures and initials, as well as several stamps and seals. All correspond to real people who held real positions on Khamene'i's staff as of the time the letter was theoretically written and delivered. Furthermore, the language is convincing; it is precisely the sort of flowery, formal language that the bureaucrats of the Islamic Republic use to correspond with one another.

Nonetheless, even some people who would benefit enormously if the letter were accepted as real had doubts about its veracity. First is the date. If anyone were inclined to forge such a letter, they would be sure to pick a date close enough to September 11 to drive policy makers to the conclusion that Iran was probably involved in the plot. Many analysts asked openly if the letter weren't "too good to be true."

Second was the background: half a year earlier a very similar letter was circulated, and most experts concluded that it was a forgery, probably constructed by the Iraqi-sponsored terrorist group, the Mujahedin E-Qalq. Still, the Mujahedin had often been the source of accurate information in the past, including details of Iran's secret nuclear program. So even if the Mujahedin were identified as the source of the letter, it would not automatically prove that it was a forgery, although it would certainly taint it.

As of this writing, the matter was still under debate. However, Iran's meddling in Iraq was not doubtful, nor was the fact that the mullahs were getting very close to having an atomic bomb.

It's hard to get accurate information on such matters—the United States has typically been surprised at the speed with which countries develop nuclear weapons, and just a few years ago the Clinton folks were astonished at an Indian nuclear test—but there are many straws in the wind suggesting that there may not be much time before the Iranians announce success. In early 2003, Georgian President Shevardnadze held a press conference in which he announced that his country's leading nuclear experts were in Iran, working on the mullahs' bomb. And last year the American government was informed of many details of the Iranian program, including a then-secret heavy water project in Arak. This operation had been hidden by a Tehran company called Masbah Energy, located on a side street just off the main drag—Vali Assra, formerly Pahlavi Avenue.

The United States was told that the chief engineers of the Arak project had come from the former Soviet Union: Vladimir Mirny of the Ukraine, Aleksy Volev of Russia, and a third expert with the catchy name of Andrei Kalachnikov.

In February or March 2003, leaders of Iran's Revolutionary Guards were informed by the country's National Security Council that the country would soon have nuclear weapons, and there are some well-informed people who tell me that the regime is hoping to be able to test a device by the end of the summer.

There is no doubt that the leaders of Iran's shaky mullahcracy view nuclear weapons as an insurance policy, both against American action and against their own alienated masses. Supreme Leader Khamene'i and his henchman, former President Rafsanjani, have spoken openly about their desire to join the nuclear club. Rafsanjani even went so far as to announce that the minute Iran had the bomb, it would be dropped on Israel, regardless of the consequences. Even if all Iranians were killed in the war, he said, it would be a good deal for Islam: half the world's Jews would be wiped out, but only a small fraction of the planet's Muslims would perish.

Perhaps such words are sheer bravado, perhaps not. But the regime is convinced by the North Korean "model" that nuclear weapons are a reliable shield against American power, and that view is shared by many strategic analysts.

I wonder if it is true. If we are convinced that democratic countries—with or without nuclear weapons—are far less likely to threaten us than tyrannies are, it may well be that a tyranny with nuclear weapons is a more urgent target for democratic revolution than one with only conventional weapons.

Perhaps a nuclear Iran requires our attention even more than a conventional Iran.

Nuclear weapons may protect the mullahs against an invasion, but they will not protect the Islamic Republic against their own people, which is the greatest threat to their tyrannical rule. Paradoxically, the more we believe that Iran is on the verge of a nuclear breakthrough, the more we should be inclined to act in accordance with President Bush's oft-repeated message that the United States supports the Iranian people's desire to be free.

To be sure, many of our finest Iran-watchers, including the great Bernard Lewis, believe that any future Iranian government, even a democratic one, is likely to continue the nuclear program. But even if it is true, a democratic Iran will not be inclined to commit hara-kiri by launching a nuclear first strike against Israel, nor would it be likely to brandish its bombs against the United States.

The combination of mounting evidence of an Iranian alliance with Al Qaeda, the murder of Americans in Saudi Arabia, and the threat of an Iranian nuclear weapon brought the policy debate in Washington to a head in late May and early June. High-level meetings were scheduled for the last week in May, and unfortunate bureaucrats were forced to cancel dinner and travel plans for the Memorial Day weekend in order to respond to more than three dozen pages of queries from the National Security Council.

The sense of urgency conveyed by such extraordinary requests demonstrates the long-standing failure of the National Security Council to either forge a consensus among the various agencies involved in national security, or to take the disagreements to the president so that he could tell them what he wanted. Our Iraq mission was defined shortly after September 11, but we still do not have an Iran policy.

Still, the urgent tasking of the national security agencies showed that even the dreamers in the Department of State and the intelligence community could no longer shrug off (or blame on ourselves) the active involvement of the mullahs in the most recent terrorist attacks, their frantic and apparently increasingly successful race to develop an atomic bomb, and their commitment of thousands of men and millions of dollars to sabotage our efforts to bring an orderly and free society to Iraq. The operation in Riyadh was planned in Iran by Al Qaeda leaders, notably Said bin Laden (Osama's son) and Mohammed Shoghi, whose nom de guerre is Abu Khalid Sayef al Adel (which means "the sword of justice"). Three days before the Riyadh attacks, seventeen Al Qaeda members were quietly moved to the Sistan and Baluchistan areas at the Pakistan border, hoping to conceal the Iranian connection, but it was uncovered anyway.

Despite all this, the dreamers continued to pursue the mirage of a miraculous accord with the mullahs. The State Department, driven by Policy Planning's Richard Haass, had eagerly sought to establish a "dialogue" with the butchers of Tehran, an effort that received full support from the NSC's man on Afghanistan and Iran, Zalmay Khalizhad, who personally conducted many of the secret talks. The very idea of "dialogue" was a triumph of American naïveté over evidence, and the Iranians eagerly exploited the talks to forestall any American move against the Tehran regime, which is the mullahs' constant nightmare. They know the Iranian people hate them (a general strike was called for the ninth of July). Both the tyrants and the citizens believe that American policy could determine the destiny of the country, as it has several times in the recent past. The mullahs used the fact of the talks to delay any American action, and to discourage the opposition. "You see," they said, "the Americans deal with us, they recognize our legitimacy. They will never support you."

If the United States chose to give real support to the regime's opponents, there could well be a replay of the mass demonstrations that led to the fall of Milosevic in Yugoslavia and the Marcoses in the Philippines. If the Bush Administration instead fell back on merely repeating the president's many words of condemnation of the regime and praise for the opposition, the mullahs would likely survive to kill us yet another day.

It is impossible to win in Iraq or to block the spread of weapons of mass destruction throughout the terror network without bringing down the mullahs. Iran is not only a participant on the other side; it is the heart of the jihadist structure. If we are really serious about winning the war against terrorism, we must defeat Iran. Thus far, we haven't been serious enough.

The debate on Iran policy must produce coherence throughout the administration. The president has been exceptionally clear about Iran—a self-appointed, terrorist-supporting tyranny with an impotent group of elected officials masking the true nature of the regime—but some of his top underlings have openly contradicted him. The dangerous confusion generated when Deputy Secretary of State Richard Armitage called Iran a "democracy" played directly into the hands of the mullahs. Top officials have to speak with a single voice.

Second, it is long past time to support the many independent Farsi-language radio and television stations that broadcast to Iran from the United States. There is an "official" American station, Radio Farda, that does some good work, but it cannot speak to the Iranians with the same authenticity as the Iranian-Americans. Senator Sam Brownback introduced legislation to accomplish this, and received considerable bipartisan support.

Third, we need to use Iraqi Shi'ism against Tehran. The Shi'ite tradition long insisted upon separation of mosque and state, but this tradition was abandoned by Iran's fanatical Ayatollah Khomeini, the leader of the anti-shah revolution of 1979. The most important Iraqi Shi'ite clerics (and a surprising number of leading Iranian ayatollahs) are opposed to the Khomeneist doctrine, and we should support them, both in Iraq and in Iran itself. The Islamic Republic has been a catastrophe for the Iranian people, ruining the economy, murdering or torturing those secular and religious leaders who call for greater freedom, shamefully enriching a handful of mullahs while prostitution, drug addiction, and beggary spread like epidemics throughout the society, and spending tens of millions of dollars to create and support the most vicious terrorist organizations, from Al Qaeda to Hizbollah.

Fourth, we need to find ways to get tangible support to the brave people who have called for a general strike in early July. Once upon a time, they could have counted on receiving money, communications equipment, and moral support from Western trade unions, private philanthropies, and their own diaspora. At the moment, none of these has been willing to join the cause, to their great shame. But if the issue were clearly defined by all the administration's leaders, miracles might be accomplished.

This is not, as so many of the administration's critics would have it, a call for further military action. Indeed, it is a prerequisite for limiting further fighting and safeguarding the lives of our soldiers now exposed to Iranian terrorism and insurrection in Iraq. It would reinforce the president's basic insight that the war against terrorism is fundamentally a struggle against tyranny, and that we have entered the Middle East as liberators, not conquerors.

The war against terrorism was never limited to a single country, or to a single strategy. We have defeated Saddam, now we must spread freedom to the heartland of the terror masters in Iran. If we do, we will find it much easier to deal with Syria and Saudi Arabia. If we fail to act decisively, we will permit the mullahs to define the near future, and we will have lost a major battle in the war.

ACKNOWLEDGMENTS AND
A NOTE ON SOURCES

Many of the best-informed people will only be helpful if they are not identified, and I have respected their desire for anonymity. That said, however, the real issue is not the identity of the sources, but their reliability. Lots of high-level anonymous sources have misled writers. I've tried hard to check the information, and I have a limited advantage, having spent some years working on counterterrorism for the American government, writing about it as a foreign correspondent for *The New Republic* and as a scholar at the American Enterprise Institute, and having made acquaintances and friends in many countries who have followed terrorism more attentively than I have. Once I decide that the information is reliable, I simply claim it as my own. If I have gotten some things wrong—and I expect I have, given the nature of the material—it's on me.

Since our government has long been poorly informed on terrorism, I have gone elsewhere for much of the information in this book. I got a lot of help from old and new friends and acquaintances here and overseas, in and out of government. I'm grateful to them all.

I'm fortunate to have exceptional literary agents and a great editor. Thanks to the three of them: Lynn Chu and Glen Hartley of Writers' Representatives, Inc., and Mac Talley at St. Martin's Press.

Professor Bernard Lewis has been good enough to spend time with me over the years, and I am most grateful for his personal guidance as well as his many published works. Reuel Gerecht of the American Enterprise Institute explained many things I had not known, and caught several errors in early drafts. Harold Rhode, at the Pentagon's Office of Net Assessments, has been my guru on the Middle East for nearly twenty years. His boss, Andy Marshall, has been a constant source of good ideas and good humor. David Wurmser, formerly at AEI and now at the Department of State, read an early draft and helped improve it. Charlie Allen, at the CIA, was one of the first people to take terrorism seriously and taught me a lot, and Dewey Clarridge, who created the CIA's Counterterrorism Center, and is now in active retirement, made several helpful suggestions.

Those of us who are fortunate enough to work at AEI know that our work would not be possible without the wisdom and support of our president, Chris DeMuth, and our vice president, David Gerson.

I received important research assistance from Daniel Aires, Olivia Ricchi, and Lauren Di Cecio.

As always, my deepest debt is to Barbara Ledeen, the love of my life, for all the wonderful things she does.

ENDNOTES

Introduction

[1] Alexis de Tocqueville, *Democracy in America* (New York, Alfred A. Knopf, 1972), Vol. II, pg. 268.

[2] Ibid., Vol. I, pg. 243.

[3] Oriana Fallaci, *La Rabbia e L'Orgoglio* (Milano: Rizzoli, 2001), pp. 71–72.

The Rise of the Terror Network

[1] Walter Laqueur, *Terrorism* (London: Abacus, 1978), pg. 40.

[2] Ibid, pg. 146.

[3] Cuba served as a Soviet proxy in South and Central America.

[4] There is a substantial literature on Soviet support for terrorism, but it is still hard to improve on Claire Sterling's *The Terror Network* (New York: Holt Rinehart & Winston, 1981). Additional documentation from the

archives of the Soviet Communist Party's Politburo can be found in Vladimir Bukovsky, *Jugement a Moscou: Un Dissident dans les Archives du Kremlin* (Paris: Robert Laffont, 1995).

[5] Khomeini's idea first came to Western attention in two books: *Islamic Government*, in Arabic (1970), and *Khomeini and His Movement* in Farsi (1975). For longer quotations and a fuller discussion, cf. Michael A. Ledeen and William Lewis, *Debacle: The American Failure in Iran* (New York: Knopf, 1980), pp. 106 ff.

[6] Shades of Mohammed Atta's will, in which he stipulates that no women are to be permitted at his funeral.

[7] Fouad Ajami, *The Vanished Imam: Musa al Sadr and the Shia of Lebanon* (Ithaca: Cornell University Press, 1986), pg. 174.

[8] Martin Kramer, "Syria's Alawis and Shi'ism," unpublished paper, cited by Ajami, loc. cit.

[9] David Wurmser, "The Saudi Connection; Osama bin Laden's a Lot Closer to the Saudi Royal Family Than You Think," in the *Weekly Standard* (October 29, 2001).

[10] The site was located at www.geocities.com/al_anssar/index.html. It was suddenly closed in mid-February 2002, after a reference to it appeared in a London-based Arabic publication.

[11] Elias Canetti, *Crowds and Power* (New York: Seabury Press, 1978), pg. 141.

[12] The dimensions of the terror universe are invariably shocking to those who haven't followed the literature.

Shortly after September 11, for example, Ulrich Kersten, the head of the BKA, Germany's FBI, said that an estimated seventy thousand terrorists were trained in bin Laden's Afghan camps alone. Cf. *Financial Times*, November 28, 2001.

13 Reuel Gerecht, "The Encyclopedia of Terror," in *Middle East Quarterly* (Summer 2001).

14 Ibid.

15 Cf., for example, Norah Vincent, "A Cult by Any Other Name: Al Qaeda," in the *Los Angeles Times*, November 29, 2001.

16 Abu 'Ubeid Al-Qurashi, "Fourth-Generation Wars," op. cit.

17 Bernard Lewis has written extensively on this important question. See his *What Went Wrong?* (London & New York: Oxford University Press, 2002).

18 Bernard Lewis, "What Went Wrong with Muslim Civilization?" in *Atlantic Monthly* (January 2002).

19 Bernard Lewis, "The Roots of Muslim Rage," in *Atlantic Monthly* (September 1990).

20 Stephen Schwartz, "This Business All Began in Saudi Arabia," in *The Spectator* (London, October 2001). Cf. also Joshua Teitelbaum, *Holier Than Thou: Saudi Arabia's Islamic Opposition* (Washington: The Washington Institute for Near East Policy, 2000).

21 Suzan Fraser, "Turkey Accuses Saudis Over Culture," *AP Online*, January 7, 2002.

22 Wurmser, op. cit.

[23] James Risen, "Bin Laden Sought Iran as an Ally, U.S. Intelligence Documents Say," in *The New York Times*, December 31, 2001.

[24] The CIA at first tried to deny the Israeli account. It took them well over a week to admit that the Iran-PLO connection was real, and then they argued that it was a brand-new development. In fact, it had been running for more than thirty years. But by March 2002, CIA chief George Tenet informed Congress that Shi'ites and Sunnis were working closely together within the terror network.

[25] David Graves and Neil Tweedie, "Allied Dossier Links Saddam to al-Qa'eda" in the *Daily Telegraph*, March 9, 2002, pg. 19.

The Home Front

[1] Ellen Harris, *Guarding the Secrets: Palestinian Terrorism and a Father's Murder of His Too-American Daughter* (New York: Scribner's, 1995), pg. 20.

[2] Ibid., pg. 265.

[3] Ibid., pg. 187.

[4] Laurie Mylroie, *A Study of Revenge: Saddam Hussein's Unfinished War Against America* (Washington, D.C.: AEI Press 2001) pp. 95–96.

[5] New guidelines to ensure better information sharing among American governmental agencies and their counterparts in allied governments were instituted by the Justice Department in mid-April 2002.

[6] Oliver Revell, "Counter-terrorism and Democratic Values: An American Practitioners Experience," delivered to the Ethics and Public Policy Center, Washington, D.C., October 11, 1996.

[7] Cf. Laurie Mylroie, op. cit., especially the introduction.

[8] Cf. Steven Emerson, *American Jihad* (New York: The Free Press, 2002).

[9] Yehudit Barsky, "Focus on Hamas: Terror by Remote Control," in *Middle East Quarterly*, June, 1996.

[10] Yigal Carmon was a founder of the Middle East Media Research Institute. See www.memri.org.

[11] Emerson, *American Jihad*, cit., pg. 106.

[12] V. S. Naipaul, *Beyond Belief* (New York: Vintage Books, 1999), pg. xi.

[13] Jerry Seper, "Clinton White House Axed Terror-Fund Probe," in the *Washington Times*, March 2, 2002, pg. 1.

[14] Machiavelli, *The Art of War*, Ch. 7. For a fuller discussion of Clinton as an example of Machiavelli's indolent prince, cf. Michael A. Ledeen, *Machiavelli on Modern Leadership* (New York: St. Martin's Press, 1998).

[15] Shortly after being nominated for the position of director of Central Intelligence, Woolsey was approached by one of Clinton's political advisors and was urged to hire one of the Clintons' Arkansas cohorts for a high position at the CIA. Woolsey flatly rejected the suggestion, and the coolness between him and the president may well have been related to Woolsey's refusal to place a Clinton insider in a sensitive intelligence post.

ENDNOTES

The Foreign Theater

[1] Michael Ledeen, "Tinker, Turner, Sailor, Spy," in *New York Magazine*, March 3, 1980, pp. 37–38.

[2] Duane R. Clarridge, *A Spy For All Seasons: My Life in the CIA* (New York: Scribner's, 1997), pg. 334.

[3] Ibid., pg. 321.

[4] Ibid., pg. 336.

[5] Best of all, it remained secret until Clarridge provided some of the details in his book. Previously the self-destruction of Abu Nidal remained a mystery. His biographer, Patrick Seale, blamed it on the Israeli Mossad. Cf. *Abu Nidal: A Gun for Hire* (New York: Random House, 1992).

[6] No doubt Reuel Gerecht has it right ("The Counterterrorist Myth," in *The Atlantic Monthly*, July/August 2001): "The CIA could find common ground with Palestinian militants, who often drink, womanize and spend time in nice hotels . . . Still, its 'penetrations' of the PLO . . . were essentially emissaries from Yasser Arafat to the U.S. government."

[7] Reuel Marc Gerecht, "The Counterterrorist Myth," in *The Atlantic Monthly*, July/August, 2001.

[8] Robert Baer, *See No Evil: The True Story of a Ground Soldier in the CIA's War on Terrorism* (New York: Crown, 2002), pg. 267.

[9] Ibid., pg. 264.

[10] *The New York Times* filed a Freedom of Information Act

request with the CIA for the Mitrokhin documents that deal with KGB operations in the United States, but the Agency turned it down, even though the Italian government actually published the Mitrokhin documents concerning Italy. The *Times* has appealed the CIA turndown.

[11] Thomas Powers, "The Trouble with the CIA," in the *New York Review of Books*, January 17, 2002.

[12] "For a 'Pearl Harbor' Inquiry," in the *Washington Post*, February 17, 2002, pg. B7.

[13] *The Counterterrorist Myth*, op. cit.

[14] Cf., for example, the account in the London *Sunday Times*, "US Missed Three Chances to Seize Bin Laden," January 6, 2002. Cf. also a firsthand account from the intermediary for two of the failed initiatives: Mansoor Ijaz, "Clinton Let Bin Laden Slip Away and Metastasize; Sudan offered up the terrorist and data on his network. The then-president and his advisors didn't respond," in *Los Angeles Times*, December 5, 2001, Part 2, pg. 13.

[15] Ruth Wedgwood, "The Law at War: How Osama Slipped Away," in *The National Interest*, Winter 2001/02, pg.70. A "must read."

[16] "US Missed Three Chances to Seize Bin Laden," op. cit.

[17] It was Bob Baer's operation, and he tells the infuriating story in his *See No Evil*, op. cit., pp. 171 ff.

How to Win the War

[1] Reuel Gerecht, "The Gospel According to Osama bin Laden," in *The Atlantic Monthly* (January 2002), p. 46.

[2] There may be a way to deter suicide terrorists, but it is so politically incorrect it is hard to imagine its adoption. The British in India faced a Muslim insurrection, and they responded by defiling the bodies of dead terrorists: The cadavers were buried in pigskin shrouds, which the Muslims believed barred them from paradise. The insurrection ended in short order. A group of Israelis buried a Palestinian terrorist in pigskin in February 2002, but it does not seem to have caught on, so its current efficacy can't be evaluated.

[3] *Jane's Foreign Report* (October 2000)

[4] Cf. Roger Highfield, "Al-Qa'eda's Atom Plans Were Spoof Science," in the *Telegraph*, November 20, 2001.

[5] Arthur M. Schlesinger Jr., on the Op-Ed page of the *Los Angeles Times*, September 23, 2001.

[6] James S. Robbins, "Overthrowing Saddam: How He Rules," in *National Review Online*, January 8, 2002.

[7] "The Saudi Connection: Osama bin Laden's a Lot Closer to the Saudi Royal Family Than You Think," in *The Weekly Standard*, October 29, 2001.

[8] David Rose, "Iraq's Arsenal of Terror," in *Vanity Fair* (May 2, 2002).

[9] James Hackett, "The Reason to Single Out Iraq," in the *Washington Times*, February 24, 2002.

[10] Ibid.

11 "Bashar Assad Teaches Visiting Members of U.S. Congress How to Fight Terrorism—Syrian Style," in MEMRI, *Special Dispatch—Syria*, January 16, 2002.

12 Michael Evans, "Al-Qaeda in Secret Talks with Lebanon Terror Group," in the *London Times*, February 1, 2002.

13 Meyrav Wurmser, *The Schools of Ba'athism: A Study of Syrian Schoolbooks* (Washington, D.C.: The Middle East Media Research Institute, 2000), pg. 37.

14 From *Islamic Education for the Fourth Grade, 1998–1999*, cited in ibid., pg. 38.

15 *Islamic Education for the Ninth Grade, 1999–2000*, cited in ibid., pg. 41.

16 Middle East Research Institute, "Terror in America (14): Syria's Position: Define Terrorism Not Fight It," October 7, 2001.

17 James Risen and Tim Weiner, "A Nation Challenged: Collaboration: C.I.A. Is Said to Have Sought Help From Syria," in *The New York Times*, October 29, 2001, pg. B3.

18 Alan Sipress and Colum Lynch, "U.S. Avoids Confronting Syrians on Iraqi Oil," in the *Washington Post*, February 14, 2002, pg. A1.

19 Quoted in Charles M. Sennott, "Doubts Are Cast on the Viability of Saudi Monarchy for Long Term," in the *Boston Globe*, March 5, 2002.

20 www.PBS.org-Frontline: Saudi Time Bomb?: interviews: vali nasr 2/12/02

21 MEMRI, "Saudi Government Daily: Jews Use Teenagers' Blood for 'Purim' Pastries" (March 13, 2002).

22 Ralph Peters, "The Saudi Threat," in the *Wall Street Journal*, January 4, 2002.

23 David Wurmser, "The Saudi Connection: Osama bin Laden's a Lot Closer to the Saudi Royal Family Than You Think," in the *Weekly Standard*, October 29, 2001.

24 Judy Dempsey, "Raid on Agency in Bosnia Points to al-Qaeda Link," in the *Financial Times Online*, February 21, 2002. The story ran in most leading printed newpapers the following day.

25 The book is called *To Be A Saudi* and will be published in the fall of 2002 by Janus Press. Cf. M. S. Ahmed, "Saudi Society Slowly Collapsing: Saudi Scion Calls for Radical Changes in the Kingdom," in www.muslimedia. com/archives/oaw98/hani.htm

Final Thoughts

1 Luigi Barzini, *From Caesar to the Mafia: Persons, Places and Problems in Italian Life* (Second Edition, London and New Brunswick, Transaction, 2002), pp. 24–25.

The Overthrow of Saddam Hussein

1 It should have been obvious to reporters that the demonstrations were manipulated from Tehran. Many demonstrators carried huge portraits of Hossein, the famous

Shi'ite martyr. Those portraits were traditional Iranian icons, and were not part of Iraq Shi'ite celebrations. The script on those portraits was Farsi, not Arabic. And common sense should have suggested the same conclusion: Iraqis had no water, no food, no electricity, and very little security. Why should anyone believe that the demonstrators had decided that the most important thing for them to do was to carefully letter some banner for an anti-American demonstration?

[2] It may seem fanciful to suggest that our liberation of Iraq could be transformed into a pro-Iranian regime applying Shariah law, but in 2002 our negotiators, headed by the NSC's Zal Khalizhad, permitted the creation of an Islamic Republic in Afghanistan. And Dr. Khalizhad, who had approved the participation of the Iranian-sponsored "opposition group" headed by the Ayatollah Bakr Hakim (who had spent twenty years in Iran and was clearly their agent), was given primary responsibility for Iran by National Security Adviser Rice in May 2003. Along with his counterparts in the State Department, Khalizhad expanded secret contacts with the Iranian regime until the Iranians were caught providing support to the Al Qaeda group that carried out the suicide bombings in Saudi Arabia in the spring of 2003.

INDEX

INDEX

Central Intelligence Agency (CIA)
  (*continued*)
  and nature of terrorist network, 45–
    48
  organization of, 100–102
  recruitment of, 100, 107, 121
  scandals in, 98, 104, 120–22
  self-destruction of, 122–26
  Soviet-Afghani war and, 37
  Soviet moles in, 115–18
  and winning war against terrorism,
    185–87, 194–95, 198, 218, 249
Chalabi, Ahmed, 140–41, 185–86,
  254, 256, 261
China, People's Republic of, 22, 43,
  49–50, 58, 230, 262
Chirac, Jacques, 144, 242–43, 244–45
Christians, 12, 30–31, 33–34, 52, 133,
  153, 198
Christopher, Warren, 188
Church, Frank, 67, 96
Clarridge, Dewey, 122, 126
  foreign security and, 102–4
Clinton, Bill, ix–x, 11, 19, 29, 44, 46
  domestic security and, 66, 83–93
  foreign security and, 115–17, 121,
    125–29, 131–37, 141–42, 250, 253
  and winning war against terrorism,
    178, 185–86
Cold War, x, xvi, xxii, 53, 79, 211–12, 214
  U.S. foreign security and, 95, 123
  and winning war against terrorism,
    148–50, 154–55, 168, 200, 216
Cole, U.S.S., terrorist attack on, 6, 84,
  134, 203
Congress, U.S., 93–94
  domestic security and, 67–72, 94
  foreign security and, 96, 98–99, 106–
    7, 111, 113, 115, 120–22, 143,
    235–36, 255
  and winning war against terrorism,
    188–89
Customs Service, 61–62

Defense Department, U.S., 255
Denmark, 240
Deutch, John, ix–xi, 93
  foreign security and, 118–21
Din, Samir Hasan Naim al-, 126

Egypt, 21
  bin Laden and, 36, 41–43
  U.S. foreign security and, 108, 128

and winning war against terrorism,
  155–56, 166, 205–6, 259
Egyptian Islamic Jihad (EIJ), 41–42,
  155–56
El Salvador, 70
Emerson, Steven, 72, 75
Encyclopedia of the Afghan Jihad, The,
  23–24, 173
Erwa, Elatih, 128–29
European Union, 243, 244–45, 279

Fahd, King of Saudi Arabia, 200, 202
Faisa, Turki al, 202
Fallaci, Oriana, ix, xix–xx, 220
Federal Aviation Administration
  (FAA), 63–64, 236
Federal Bureau of Investigation (FBI),
  xxiii
  congressional investigations of, 67–
    72, 96, 98, 113
  domestic security and, 54–56, 58–
    60, 62–74, 76–77, 81, 86–87, 94,
    234–35
  foreign security and, 115–17, 130,
    132, 135
  investigative restrictions on, 68–71,
    87, 98–99, 234–35
  morale of, 71–72, 74
  scandals in, 67–68, 70, 98, 120–21
  Soviet moles in, 115–16
  successes of, 59–60
Feltrinelli, Giangiacomo, 110
Finnsbury Park Mosque, 22–23
Foruhar, Dariush, 228
Foruhar, Parastoo, 228
Fourth-Generation Wars, 18
France, 241, 242, 243, 244–45, 264
Fraunces Tavern, terrorist bombing of,
  7
Freeh, Louis, 130
French Revolution, 1

Gerecht, Reuel, 95, 112, 123–24, 235
Germany, 241, 243, 264, 265, 266
Gertz, Bill, 48–49
Gorbachev, Mikhail, 149, 214, 217
Great Britain, 226, 241, 252, 255,
  256, 276
Greece, 5–7
Grenada, 149, 218
Gulf War, xvi, 157, 214–16, 241, 242
  bin Laden and, 37, 40, 212
  U.S. foreign security and, 139–40

INDEX

INDEX

INDEX

INDEX